The Norfolk
Walker's Book

DEDICATION

To those who walk Norfolk's byways, and to those
who may soon begin.

I know not where the white road runs,
Nor what the blue hills are,
But a man can have the sun for friend,
And for his guide a star.
And there's no end of voyaging when
Once the voice is heard,
For the rivers call, and the road calls,
And oh! the call of a bird!

(by Gerald Gould[106], 1885-1936)

The Norfolk Walker's Book

A passing glance at our roadside heritage

Bruce Robinson

Elmstead Publications

Wicklewood, Norfolk, NR18 9QL

Published 1998

© Bruce Robinson

Elmstead Publications, Elmstead, Milestone Lane, Wicklewood, Norfolk, NR18 9QL

First Published 1998

ISBN: 0 9523379 2 4

British Library Cataloguing in Publication Data. A catalogue record for this book is available from the British Library.

Text input and book design by the author using a DTP system with PageMaker 5. Main text font: Times Roman.

Printed by Geo. Reeve Ltd, Wymondham, Norfolk. NR18 0BD

All photographs and maps by Bruce Robinson. Front cover picture: path to the church at Hackford, near Hingham; and silhouette of walkers on a stile near Mulbarton.

Foreword, ever forward

There's more to walking that meets the eye and here Bruce takes us on a refined ramble through the centuries to add spice to our treks through the wonderful Norfolk countryside of today. He has been more than just a good companion on our long distance walks together. He is a mine of information as we plod along, and I expect at any moment to be overtaken by a century of Roman infantry or have to leap into a ditch to avoid a speeding Iceni chariot. Taking to the not-so-flatlands of Norfolk is something everyone should try to experience, for it is only along the footpaths, green lanes and byways that you discover the true character and delights of this county of contrasts. And walking is the surest method of discovery, for not even astride a bicycle can you catch those hidden gems of the rural landscape. Even an area so familiar to you as you drive can come alive when you put on your walking boots. This book is a journey through time, making many calls along the way - some long, some short, but all informative. It will help you as you walk to fill your imagination with what has been and so take your mind off what is to come. Personally, I would have found it useful on the awful stretch of the Peddars Way from Castle Acre to Shepherd's Bush - three and a half miles of rising Tarmac stretching, it seems, in the direction of eternity. I'm sure it would have helped had I realised that not so many years ago most countryfolk walked everywhere they needed to go. They would have dismissed my protestations as trivial, with three and a half miles being but a stroll at a time when walking was a necessity, while now it is a pleasurable pastime. Bruce has found a mass of fascinating facts and woven them into a tapestry of time, from prehistory to the present, making this volume a very readable companion whether you be a walker or not. If you are inspired to become a walker when you will find the final chapter devoted to the 'ups and downs' and 'dos and don'ts' for long distance trekkers. Here, Bruce gives sound advice after many lessons learned. And I'm happy to say we learned a great deal of them together along the way.

David Williams

Contents

Contents

By the same author:

A History of Long Sutton (South Lincolnshire).
Produced privately, 1965 (with F W Robinson).
The Peddars Way. The Weathercock Press, 1978.
A Skylark Descending (novel). Robert Hale, 1978.
History of Long Sutton & District. Long Sutton Civic
Trust, 1981 (with F W Robinson). Reprinted 1995.
Norfolk Origins 1: Hunters to First Farmers. Acorn
Editions, 1981 (with Andrew Lawson).
Norfolk Origins 2: Roads & Tracks. Poppyland
Publishing, 1983 (with Edwin Rose).
The Peddars Way and Norfolk Coast Path. Countryside
Commission, 1986.
Norfolk Origins 3: Celtic Fire & Roman Rule.
Poppyland Publishing, 1987 (with Tony Gregory).
Peddars Way and Norfolk Coast Path. Aurum Press,
1992. Reprinted 1996.
Norfolk Fragments. Elmstead Publications, 1994.
A Glimpse of Distant Hills (novel). Elmstead Publications
1995.
Chasing the Shadows: Norfolk Mysteries Revisited.
Elmstead Publications, 1996.
Passing Seasons: a watching brief on 50 years of football.
Elmstead Publications, 1997.

At various intervals throughout this book, and
accompanying the text, you will find information
Sidelines such as this one. Each has the open book
logo as a prefix, for easy reference. They are designed
to supply additional information specific to the subject
being discussed in the text. All the Sidelines, and the
subjects, are listed on the Contents page.

Introduction

It is necessary to explain what this book is about, because it does not give the intimate details of a single walk. First, it is to celebrate the call of the open road, a concept as nebulous as any I have ever attempted to pin down; but a worthy one, nonetheless. Second, it is to enlighten and entertain the mature (though not necessarily expert) walker whose pace, like mine, has slowed but who still possesses a pair of boots and who occasionally wonders, in passing, why some roads are straight and others are not. A third reason is a desire to provide walkers with a sort of handbook which may help to explain some of the things they see or do not understand. There are many categories not included and some, such as trees, flowers, birds and churches, which have been dealt with only in the briefest terms. My excuses are ignorance and the fact that good books on these subjects have already been published by others. In addition - and I suppose this is a fourth reason - I have written it in the hope that it might actually persuade someone who, up to the moment, has only thought of going on a long walk, to get out and do it. Incidentally, figures in parenthesis inserted in the text indicate a reference or a book listed in the References and Bibliography section at the end. This is my fifth attempt at self-publication and once again a long list of people are waiting to be thanked, among them current walking and former work colleague David Williams, for his kind Foreword; the many walking companions who over the years have accompanied me along the Peddars Way, the Coast Path, Angles Way and Weavers' Way; all the past and present members of the several unofficial Eastern Counties Newspapers' editorial walking groups; and the staff of George Reeve Ltd, Wymondham, who once again kept me - technologically speaking - on the straight and narrow.

Bruce Robinson

The Peddars Way near North Pickenham.

Call of the Road

I love roads:
The goddesses that dwell
Far along invisible
Are my favourite gods.

Roads go on
While we forget, and are
Forgotten like a star
That shoots and is gone.

(From the poem Roads, by Edward Thomas, 1878-1917)

t some point during that period of artificial calm before the First World War the writer and poet Edward Thomas observed that whereas a great deal had been written about travel far less had been said of the road. He was right in a sense that then - and some would add, as now - books about travel, or the charms of nature and the countryside, proliferated, whereas titles relating to the actual history of those same lanes and paths might be counted on very few fingers. It was left, among others, to Sidney Webb (The Story of the King's Highway, 1906), Hilaire Belloc,[3] and to Thomas himself, who subsequently wrote affectionately and informatively of the Icknield Way,[4] to attempt to rectify matters. There were a number of reasons for this evident imbalance. Kim Taplin[5] pointed out that most written references to footpaths occurred in the 19th and 20th centuries, first, because rural England in pre-Industrial times was unenclosed and access to the countryside was more general and commonplace, and second, because pre-Industrial literature tended to view the landscape from the standpoint of the owners of great houses who, by implication, had little occasion to walk the paths. In other

Competitive walking, known as 'heel and toe' - still seen in walking races today - had its heyday in the late 18th and early 19th centuries. Most solo contests involved time and distance, given added impetus by large wagers. Standard distances [105] were five, 10, 50, 100 and 1000 miles. Roads with milestones, parks, commons and race courses were used. The competitors were popularly known as 'peds.' The most famous 'pedestrians' were Capt Agar, Levi Bramham, and George Wilson, who walked 1000 miles in 20 days. In 1773 Foster Powell walked from London to York and back, covering the 402 miles in just over five days and 15 hours. He duly became a national hero, and four years later walked from London to Canterbury and back in 24 hours. The most famous was Capt Barclay, who regularly walked 30 miles before breakfast. In 1801 he made a third attempt to walk 90 miles in just over 21 hours, for 5000 guineas, and finished with an hour to spare. The big challenge was to walk 1000 miles in 1000 continuous hours, but the best walkers had not lasted more than 30 days. This time £100,000 was wagered, and at Newmarket at midnight on June 1, 1809, he set off, completing the distance at 3pm on July 12. Massive crowds celebrated and church bells rang. In 1851 William Gale walked 1500 miles in 1000 successive hours.

words, it was inconceivable that the 'short and simple annals of the poor,' which might have included the lore of the paths, would have been of any interest whatsoever to book-buying gentlefolk. It was also a fact that walkers were, in essence, unpopular. As Morris Marples[105] noted in 1960, when the prejudice was to an extent still apparent: 'Mankind in general has seldom regarded walking as a pleasure. No doubt it has too often been the case that to walk meant simply that a man could not afford to ride . . .'

Today, there is no practical need to walk the green lanes. They rarely go anywhere of importance or serve any real purpose, and it is certainly quicker and less tiring to travel from A to B by car. Therefore, those who take the trouble to venture along the old, green ways do so by conscious decision. And nowadays, let it be said, there are many of them. In the final decades of the 20th century leisure walking is a firmly established pastime, a revolt, partly, against regimes of concrete and air pollution, restricted access and stress, job insecurity and noise. Even so, the actual reasons for strolling or walking remain elusive, even questionable. Ask a stroller, 'Why walk?' just as a mountaineer is sometimes asked about the relevance of climbing, and the answer is usually evasive. What is more, the reasons tend to vary from person to person, so that in the end one is simply left with a rag bag of personal aspirations and intentions. However,

A walker on the Peddars Way route betwixt Merton and the Watton road.

some generalities do surface with a certain inevitability. Relaxation. Fresh air. Exercise. Companionship. Pubs. Nature. The Countryside. A need to 'get away,' to leave worry and routine behind. But a perceptive Mike Harding[104] observed that if you do ask a 'bog standard rambler' why he does it he will indeed mutter something about fresh air and exercise, leading Harding to opine that 'this is just a cover-up . . . They are playing truant. That simply is the top and bottom of it.' Ralph Waldo Emerson, on the other hand, who spoke deliciously of a walk in the woods as the 'consolation of mortal man,' also wrote entertainingly of the degrees of proficiency of walkers. 'The qualifications are endurance, plain clothes, old shoes, an eye for nature, good humour, vast curiosity, good speech, good silence, and nothing much.'[106] All of these factors are important, of course. Yet, stripped of relatively commonplace and fairly obvious observations a suspicion dawns that there must be another reason, another answer to the original question floating

The mile, so-called from the Latin mille - which in this sense means 1000 paces - is the standard measure of length in the British Commonwealth and the United States. The Roman lineal measure was 1000 paces, or between 1620 and 1611 modern English yards. Old English and Scottish miles were different again, being longer - about 2240 and 1980 yards respectively - while London once had an ancient mile of about 1666 yards. The British statute mile was legally set at 1760 yards in 1593, which means it has been measuring our progress for over 400 years.

like dark matter in many walkers' personal universe. Edward Thomas, killed by a shell blast at Arras in 1917, had a fairly earthy view. 'We walk,' he wrote,[4] 'for a thousand reasons, because we are tired of sitting, because we cannot rest ...' But I think he was only partially correct, because I also believe that buried deep there is an emotional need to walk. Given half a chance by anyone prepared to stand and listen and feel, the paths can and do exert a persuasive pull and an attraction of their own. This is what might be called the undefined, the ethereal, the Call of the Road.

Throughout the centuries there have been many reasons for walking, tramping or strolling, and it is best to acknowledge the fact. Basic walking, for want of a better phrase, might be defined as the means of getting to work and back, of travel for commercial reasons, and as a way of delivering loads. Fashionable walking, or strolling from church to park, to neighbours or to theatre, was largely the preserve of the wealthy. Then there was Competitive walking (1000 miles in 1000 hours, for example), undertaken for money, which was followed by Recreational walking, undertaken for adventure, exploration, curiosity, or religious or literary reasons. In this last category one might place RL Stevenson, Wordsworth, Coleridge, Sir Walker Scott, Laurence Sterne, Richard Jeffries, Donne, Ben Jonson, Thomas Campion, Hazlitt, George Borrow, or one of the earliest of the breed, Thomas Coryate (born about 1577), who walked from Odcombe in Somerset to Venice and back[105] and earned a living writing about it. Later, he visited Italy, but died on yet another hike, this time in India. He was later remembered by having his

walking shoes displayed in Odcombe church until the 18th century. Other early walkers included the Scot, William Lithgow, who in about 1610 and because of an ill-fated love affair made three trips to Europe, Asia Minor and North Africa, and John Taylor (born Gloucester, 1580), who wrote about his travels in verse. But even here there were shades of difference. Whereas Stevenson explored afoot in strange lands, Jeffries, the observer, was content to tread the same familiar paths year by year. Then, of course, there is also the Leisure walking of today, including hiking and touring, undertaken purely for pleasure.

What is plain is that the ploughman and the dairymaid did stroll their local green lanes to rid their lungs of dust, stretch their muscles, to relax and, inevitably, to meet. Yet it is not absolutely clear when walking, purely for rural - as opposed to urban - relaxation actually became popular. Perhaps the many strands of fashion are entwined and have become indistinguishable. In any event this new vogue implied a new and radical use of the paths. Now the green lanes and old roads were being used for pleasure and recreation and not simply for commerce, work and travel. It was a revelation. Novelist and naturalist Richard Jefferies, in his essay On the London Road,[6] probably written in the 1880s, saw something of the phenomenon, observing: 'But through this long (village) street, and on out into the open, is continually pouring the human living undergrowth of that vast forest of life, London ... For what end? Why this tramping and ceaseless movement?' Stevenson related dryly in Travels with a Donkey[7]: 'For my part, I travel not to go anywhere, but to go. I travel for travel's sake. The great affair is to move.' But the dating of this leisure revolution remains a moot point. Morris Marples,[105] in discussing the gentle art of tramping, concluded that the Boer War (1899) and the arrival of the Boy Scout movement

A threat of rain: Halvergate marsh.

The word 'road' has a niche in literature and language,[1]: all roads lead to Rome; gentlemen of the road; one for the road; on the road. Then there is travellers' tales; best foot forward; life's milestones; and Shanks's Mare/Pony. This last one seems to be a slang expression from the first half of the 18th century. It meant 'to go on foot,' the same as 'going by the marrow-bone stage,' or 'Walker's bus,' which made light of the fact that the walker could not afford the ride. According to another source[103] the word 'road' springs from the same origins as 'ride,' which in Old English meant 'riding' or 'hostile incursion on horseback,' a meaning possibly preserved in 'making inroads.' 'Path' is a West German word, while 'way', though Old English, is connected to the German and Dutch 'weg' and the Swedish 'vag.' The word 'street', borrowed from the Latin 'strata', means a road that has been 'spread,' for example, with paving stones. 'Hike' is an Old English word which became obsolete and returned to this country from America in 1926, while 'tramp,' slang in America, means 'to walk,' or a person with no home or doing casual work.

(1907) had lent impetus to a general desire to 'rough it,' to which one might suggest that memories of the First World War surely played a part, too.

Even earlier fashions helped to revive the Arcadian myth which in its simplest form represented, and still does represent, a yearning for something, a reminiscence of long ago, a green and pleasant English land, memories of things lost, rustic simplicity, thatched cottages and scented gardens. I am always reminded of it on hearing Beethoven's 6th Symphony, which we call the Pastoral but which the composer actually sub-titled, 'Pastoral Symphony or Memories of Country Life (Expression of feeling rather than illustration).' Of course, it does contain some illustration - the storm, for example - but in essence Beethoven was painting an emotional picture of the countryside. When it was first performed in Vienna in 1808 a new musical language was unveiled, for it contained an enormous surge of feeling for the countryside and for nature in an outpouring of sentiment and emotion. Kim Taplin's book The English Path[5] explored a similar point, following the literary vein and extolling in particular John Clare (1793-1864), William Barnes (1800-1886), Thomas Hardy (1840-1928), Richard Jefferies (1848-1887), John Cowper Powys (1872-1963) and, of course, Edward Thomas (1878-1917). Clearly, writers and poets looking at the landscape, perhaps for the first time, also had to invent a new language.

For centuries the paths had encompassed the familiar world of a majority of people who hardly travelled more than a few miles from home. They provided a connecting thread, a sort of 'mental landscape.' Once upon a time the paths and roads were simply used. Now they were being loved, and recognised as man's oldest mark upon the landscape. It was but a short step from there to reinvent the enduring nature of the road and the even older parallel of the road as a metaphor for life complete with hardships, pleasures, hidden corners, accidental encounters and an inevitable ending. In fact there is an appealing symmetry to the idea. RL Stevenson,[100] touching on the theme, wrote: 'It is as if we were marching with the rear of a great army, and from far before heard the acclamation of the people as the vanguard entered some friendly and jubilant city. Would not every man, through all the long miles of march, feel as if he also were within the gates?' It reminded me of a newer story that whereas British county boundaries are squiggly, American state boundaries are generally straight. The road to a better life is straight ahead. Therefore, so the story went, the Americans are optimists while the British are realists. As a story it is a little too neat, perhaps, though there is comfort in Stevenson's reference to Blake's comment in Marriage of Heaven and Hell: 'Improvement makes straight roads; but the crooked roads, without improvement, are roads of genius.'

Nevertheless, there are many ways of looking at roads and paths, and using them for inspiration and relaxation is but one. Two others, perhaps, are to travel the road and write about the experience of the journey, as Coryate did; and to stop and observe life passing by. There are numerous examples of travel books, but the ranks of passive observers and recorders, are substantially thinner. One of my favourites is The Roadmender.[8] Written by Michael Fairless and first published in 1902, it provoked something of a stir, for Michael Fairless was, in reality, Margaret Fairless Barber, born in Yorkshire in 1869. Her mother, in later life, lived (and died, in 1891) in Bungay, a place Margaret visited periodically. She herself became very ill but continued to write until her own death in 1901. Her humble stonebreaker squats beside the road working under a hedge of sapling, late roses, woodbine and sweet-brier, while nearby is a white gate through which his soul one day will pass. He watches the birds, the seasons and the passers-by, who sometimes speak and sometimes ignore him (the old widow, with whom he lodges and shares his weekly shilling; the young priest, the waggoner, the aged couple trudging towards the workhouse, tramps, a girl on a bicycle, horsemen, a funeral, a drover, the miller's wife; and so on. It ends inevitably yet confidently at the white gate: 'Farewell! It is a road mender's word; I cry you Godspeed to the next milestone - and beyond.'

Hilaire Belloc (1870-1953), in his introductory chapter on the Fascination of Antiquity,[3] touched on the subject of walking and affection for the roads and paths he trod. He and two companions trudged the old pilgrim road from Winchester to Canterbury, beginning in late December in order to reach the cathedral on the anniversary of Becket's death, and wrote afterwards: 'We are slow to feel its (the road's) influence. We take so much for granted that its original meaning escapes us. Men, indeed, whose pleasure it is perpetually to explore even their own country on foot, and to whom its every phase of climate is delightful, receive, somewhat tardily, the spirit of The Road. They feel a meaning in it . . . But for the mass The Road is silent . . .' On the other hand, perhaps it does not pay to get too carried away. CW Scott-Giles, in his introduction,[2] commented testily: 'If you seek romance it is no use looking to the physical road, its line, formation, and surroundings; for the romance of the road is a matter of association, and therefore can exist only in the mind of the traveller.'

An overgrown road sign at Deopham, near Hingham.

Is it all in the mind? Or is there, as Belloc thought, a hidden meaning? Certainly some routes have a character all of their own. As Edward Thomas observed,[4] 'Some roads creep, some continue merely; some advance with majesty ...' He also commented, with more than a grain of truth, that the more the paths are downtrodden the more they seem to flourish. Certainly roads can exert an influence of their own, engender trade and encourage travel. And they can be unforgiving in that they invariably exact a price, be it fatigue, tyre wear, discomfort, dust, delay or blisters. But are they ever to blame? 'Killer bends claim fourth victim' proclaimed a recent newspaper headline, as though the essence of the road contained a element of malevolence, or the bends were to blame for someone's speed or inattention. Mischief, yes,

On the Weaver's Way trail near Felbrigg.

where a road leads to a summit only to reveal, on achieving it, another distant summit still to be reached. But malevolence? Surely not. Can, then, an old road absorb memory? I like to think so. They can be wise, gently leading you away from or round a hazard, distilling for your individual use the wisdom of the centuries and of those who had travelled this way before, suggesting the best direction to go. Belloc[3] said: 'In climbing, the summit is nearly always hidden, and nothing but a track will save you from false journeys. In descent it alone will save you a precipice or an unfordable stream. It knows upon which side an obstacle can be passed, where there is firm land in a morass, and where there is the best going . . . It will find what nothing but long experiment can find for an individual traveller . . . and everywhere the Road, especially the very early Road, is wiser than it seems to be . . . It reminds me of those old farmers who do not read . . . but whom, if we watch closely, we shall find doing all their work just in that way which infinite time has taught the country-side.'

Stevenson[100] stressed mood and charm. Writing in 1873 he said, 'From (the road's) subtle windings and changes of level there arises a keen and continuous interest that keeps the attention ever alert and cheerful. Every sensitive adjustment to the contour of the ground, every little dip and swerve seems instinct with life and an exquisite sense of balance and beauty. The road rolls upon the easy slopes of the country like a long ship in the hollows of the sea . . . A footpath across a meadow . . . in all its human waywardness and unaccountability . . . will always be more to us than a rail-road well engineered through a difficult country.' So the traveller, he thought, was always aware of a sympathy of mood between himself and the road so travelled.

And the future? Marples[105] made the point that walking, 'like any other revolution, will proceed on its way inexorably, until some sort of an equilibrium is reached.' In which case the far horizons have still to be glimpsed. Or perhaps they are just beginning to come into view. Researcher Rainer Bramer[108] recently looked into the thorny question of what makes a landscape beautiful and concluded that, among other things, it required woods and trees (symbols of shelter), water or a lake (the life source), borders between the lake and the shore, or an open space (suggesting safety), and mountains or hills trailing into the distance (exciting curiousity). He clearly linked a beautiful landscape with calmness, and walking with science or medicine. Walk therapy beckons. Though of course, this is something regular walkers have always enjoyed.

When the moment does come to tot up the final set of accounts perhaps we will realise that infinite patience and infinite time is what our lanes and paths possess. In the past the old roads brought and took away, and helped silence the clamour of the towns. Now they beckon the unknown, enliven the imagination, evoke a remembrance of people and places, and time passing, and issue a call many of us find very hard, if not impossible, to ignore. Revere them, if you will.

Growth of the Network

he scope of subject matter in this section, which ranges from local geology to the spawning of dual carriageways, would normally demand the use of many pages in several books. Thus it will be realised that these weighty matters, which involve such considerable periods of time, are here dealt with somewhat briefly. Two further factors contribute to this, one being that the works of other writers who deal with the same, or similar, subjects are already available in bookshops and libraries. A second factor is that some of the individual categories are dealt with in more detail in Chapter 3 (Making the Difference). Thus this particular chapter is designed simply to construct a framework, to give a general impression of the terrain and landscape of Norfolk, how it came to be what it is, and how communications systems developed over the centuries.

GEOLOGY

Norfolk is perhaps best explained as a series of sedimentary deposits laid down in sequence and then tilted, so that the earliest layers are exposed in the north-west of the county, in the Hunstanton area, with some of the lowest buried deep in the east. For example, the chalk deposit which outcrops near the surface in the north-west is, in the east, more than 180 metres below Yarmouth. It gives the county a distinct list, or as a Norfolkman would say, 'Thass a bit on the huh.' Nearly all of this is due to the crushing and smoothing effects of successive sequences of ice sheets and melt waters.

During the Middle and Upper Pleistocene and Holocene geological epochs- covering roughly the last 800,000 years - there were five warm periods (interglacials; some of them warmer than today), labelled Pastonian, Cromerian, Hoxnian, Ipswichian and Flandrian, which is the one we enjoy today; and four spells of glaciation (Beestonian, Anglian, Wolstonian, and the most recent, Devensian). During the Anglian and Wolstonian glaciations Norfolk was completely covered by ice,[9] and although the end of the last glaciation (Devensian) was relatively rapid it still took 10,000 years to melt the glaciers back to their present limits. At the same time lakes were formed outside the glacier limits, including several in Norfolk. However, it was the Anglian glaciation that had such a huge influence on the soils and drainage patterns of Norfolk, on early colonisation, and subsequently on the development of agriculture.[10]

Below the till that blanketed the area during the Anglian glaciation are gravels and river deposits that indicate the former course of a huge waterway, now known as the Bytham river,[11] that once flowed north-east from the Midlands, turned east near Leicester and crossed what is now the Fens, and then swung south near what is now King's Lynn to join the ancestral Thames near Bury St Edmunds. It departed from our area roughly in the vicinity of Cromer and West Runton. This drainage system was subsequently destroyed by ice sheets, but patches of the river gravels still exist. Later, the river which ultimately became known as the Thames migrated south while the much altered Bytham river continued to flow across north-east Norfolk, leaving the present coastline somewhere between Lowestoft and Southwold. Essentially, the Bytham river seems to have provided the area's geographical framework at the time of the first known human occupation of Norfolk, possibly 500,000 years ago. The time scale was vast, but the continual glacial process of advance, melt and retreat, buried many layers of geological deposits and altered, smoothed and rippled the landscape. The familiar contours of the Norfolk we see today were primarily dictated by these and other natural forces.

Until about 6400BC Norfolk was still joined to the Continent by a coastline which stretched from North Yorkshire and round Dogger Bank to join the western shore of Jutland. The area between, the North Sea Basin, was a land of forest (pieces of which can still be picked up on the beach in the Titchwell area), swamp, and freshwater pools. Not until sea levels rose did the basin finally succumb to inundation, and Britain become an island.

Cliff erosion near Weybourne.

RIVERS and the WATERSHED
About 8000 years ago, when sea waters were inching towards Norfolk's present coastline, the drainage of fresh water,

particularly along the North Norfolk coast, was impeded. Deposits of peat began to develop. Then the incoming sea flooded the marshes. About 4500 years ago the peat forming conditions seem to have returned, and these were the deposits, at least along the Yare and the Waveney, which were exploited by medieval diggers who inadvertently helped create the present Broads. Periodically, of course, the sea attempts to re-assert its influence.

Most of Norfolk's rivers, aside from the Great Ouse, are generally of modest width and continue seawards at a leisurely pace. Early settlers tended to prefer river valleys, and when populations were low then the higher lands (interfluves) were used, perhaps seasonally, for woodland and pasture. Settlements and farms needed to be near water, while the rivers, valleys and interfluves offered defensive options. One of the last areas to be developed for farming may have been the watershed which, as defined by Tom Williamson,[12] runs in an arc north to south across Norfolk between the rivers Yare, Wensum, Waveney, Tud, Tas and others which drain towards the former estuary near Yarmouth; the Nar, Thet and Wissey which drain west towards the Wash; and the Glaven, Burn and Stiffkey, which discharge into the North Sea. The watershed seems to have been a remote area of 'reduced contact,' a social and political buffer zone where woodland was still to be found even at the time of the Domesday.

THE REGIONS
Norfolk is a blend of deep soils, muted terrain and a generally dry climate, which helps to explain why there is so much arable farming and why big fields and massive hulks of farm machinery are so popular.
Breckland (Swaffham and Thetford)
A tract of light, 'blowing' sands filling a chalk plateau, and one of the driest spots in Britain. It is also one of the most distinctive landscapes in Norfolk. Gentle slopes, sparsely populated heaths and commons and thin soils over a chalk/sand drift tend to prevail. Present land use includes pine plantations, a military training area, and large arable farms which would be considered marginal were it not for huge irrigation schemes. Fine walking country, with many needle-strewn paths among the conifer forests.
West Norfolk lowland (east of King's Lynn)
Between the chalk scarp and Fenland, an area of sandy, wet hollows; a mixed landscape cut by several rivers with villages sited on the ridges. North-south communication was always difficult, and even the Icknield Way tended to keep to the higher ground. A great deal of woodland was planted here during the last two centuries.

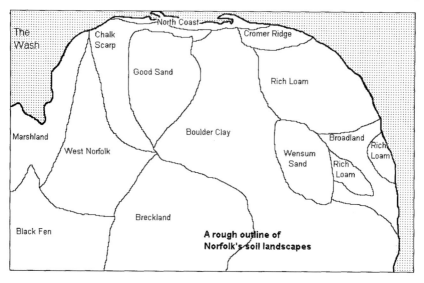

A rough outline of Norfolk's soil landscapes

Wensum sand (north and west of Norwich)
Some well drained brown sands, but a high water table. A mixture of arable, pine and deciduous woodland, with two meandering rivers and wide, green valleys.

Broadland and Flegg
Lower reaches of the Broadland rivers drain marine alluvium, and there are saltings, dunes and shingle bars. There is deep peat under reed marshes and alder carr, and a complicated system of winding valleys and marshland, natural streams and man-made drainage dykes which tend to feed the Yare, Waveney and Bure. These in turn converge on Breydon Water, all that remains of a former estuary which once stretched as far inland as Acle. Between the valleys are bands of higher land which are intensively farmed and settled.

Black fen (inland of King's Lynn)
Extensively drained, in consequence of which much peat land has been lost through shrinkage and erosion. Some of the land, which supports intensive vegetable farming, is below sea level.

Marshland (west of King's Lynn)
Estuarine silt and clay, much of it reclaimed from the Wash. Because of special water retention qualities these soils support some of the most intensively farmed arable land in the country. So productive is it, in fact, that it used to be said locally that all a man needed to make a living was 10 acres and a greenhouse. That may have been true immediately after the Second World War, but those days

have long gone. Generally held to be a walkers' no-go area because of its immediate bleakness, but this is not wholly true.

Boulder clay plateau (central Norfolk)
A broad, medium to heavy-soiled upland spanning the north-south watershed. The clay is a glacial till rich in chalk stones. Thanks to extensive drainage systems arable farms dominate. A softly undulating landscape with lots of small, local roads and straggly villages.

Rich loam (north-east Norfolk)
Well drained light to medium loam, and some of the most productive soils in the county. Particularly good at sustaining crops throughout dry spells.

Good sand (higher ground of north-west Norfolk)
So-named by agricultural writer Arthur Young, this was once an area of heaths and sheep walks, much 'improved' by modernising landowners in the 18th century. A versatile area now used for arable, grassland, and fruit and vegetable farming, embracing a tract of dry, rolling upland with the chalk either near the surface or covered by light, glacial soils. Near Docking, the chalk reaches a height of about 290ft. Nice, easy walking country.

Cromer ridge (Cromer/Holt area)
A ridge of gravel, sand and clay which includes the county's highest spot, at Beacon Hill, West Runton. Much of the escarpment is wooded, but some heaths remain. The sands and loams can cause problems of erosion.

Chalk scarp (Castle Acre to Holme)
Land use hereabouts is almost entirely arable, and dryness and erosion can be a problem on the slopes.

THE WEATHER
Norfolk is generally one of the driest areas in England, parts of Breckland receiving less than 23in a year. One reason is that prevailing westerlies shed much of their rain before they reach the east of the country. But Norfolk's coastline faces several ways at once, and sometimes suffers accordingly. Siberian winds can howl across the North Sea, while a south-westerly air stream can bring blisteringly hot spells. Spring is sometimes chilly while July can produce thunderstorms. As for the coastline areas, they tend to have micro climates all of their own. For walking holidays, I prefer May, June, September and October, but it can be good (or bad) at any time. Best to have sun hat, sweater and waterproofs close to hand.

EARLY INCURSIONS
About 500,000 years ago groups of humans began to spread into Europe, possibly from Africa or Asia, and some of them seem to have wandered as far as Britain. No

A debate over the dating of the arrival of the first humans in Norfolk has continued for many years. It centres on the Anglian glaciation, now fixed at between 478,000 and 423,000 years ago. Were humans present before ice sheets covered the area, or did they not appear until later? Excavations at Boxgrove (West Sussex) produced evidence of human activity before the Anglian stage, a fact underlined by other evidence from High Lodge, Suffolk. Below the Anglian stage deposits in Norfolk and the Midlands are the gravels and river channel deposits of the Bytham River system, and it is in these surviving patches of river gravel, at Shrub Hill (Feltwell) and Hockwold, that palaeolithic hand axes have been found. Thus it looks as if small bands of humans had penetrated the area some 500,000 years ago, before the Anglian ice sheets gripped the land, possibly camping on or near the banks of the now long vanished river. But it is still not known who they were, whether they were hunter/scavengers, or if they migrated seasonally across the North Sea basin.

skeletons have been found in Norfolk, but flint artefacts dating from before the Anglian glaciation have been discovered in sediments. More detailed evidence has come from Boxgrove, near Chichester, where in 1993 a tibia (shin bone) was uncovered. It showed the owner[13] to have been robust, heavily muscled, active, and probably around 6ft tall. Animal bones (red deer, bison, horse, rhino) scattered around suggested the area was a butchering site near a watering hole, presumably where animals came to feed and where the humans preyed upon them. One bone had been used as a hammer to make flint axes, while scratch marks on a human tooth suggested he or she held meat in their left hand, gripped it with their teeth, and then sawed it with a hand axe. The ice sheets of the Anglian glaciation period, which covered the whole of Norfolk, put an end to further incursions, but the melting of the glaciers enabled parties of humans to explore the territory again. At this time Norfolk's terrain looked much as it does today, though the rivers flowed at a higher level and the coastline was further away. Although the English Channel had been breached, a land connection with the Continent still remained.

Then history took one of its long, deep breaths and changed into an even lower gear. From the end of the Anglian glaciation and until the melting of the Devensian ice sheets (which affected only north and north-west Norfolk) small groups seem to have penetrated the area intermittently. Stone tools have been found[10] mainly in the gravels of former channels, with the most prolific sites in the valleys of the Little Ouse, the Yare and Nar - Keswick and Whitlingham, near Norwich;

Thetford and Weeting; and at South Acre. They probably lived on 'wild' vegetation and meat, and because of the chill wore clothes and built shelters. But there is very little to show for 400,000 years of intermittent human intervention.

Because of the effects of the ice sheets, and the smallness of the subsequent population, it is assumed[16] that no tracks or paths in Norfolk can be older than 10,000 years and that the earliest were probably made by animals, not humans. Then about 8300BC the cold climate of the Devensian glaciation gave way to the Mesolithic period, during which Norfolk was occupied by small groups of hunter/gatherers who made their way along the river valleys and into the open landscape. They were highly mobile and travelled huge distances, and seem to have had a lifestyle similar to Bushmen. Kelling Heath was much favoured, seeing seasonal visits over a long period of time, perhaps because from the heights of the Holt/Cromer ridge they could keep an eye on browsing herds of migratory deer and auroch (giant ox). Then in about 6500BC, as sea levels rose, the North Sea basin was inundated and Britain became an island.

FIRST FARMERS

Settled communities began to appear about 4500BC, while examples of the distinctive and delicate Mesolithic flint work begin to tail off. Whether these first farmers were descendants of the Mesolithic people is not known, but settled communities signalled a substantial change of direction. There must have been a long, anguished period during which a farming economy was slowly

In 1993 it was reported[14] that experts had unearthed a 7000BC road in County Kildare with the first known pothole, a gap worn by constant use. In the 1970s built tracks were uncovered in the Somerset Levels, including the Sweet Track, then claimed as the oldest known timber trackway. It was dated[13] to 3806BC, shown to have been used for 14 years.

The Icknield Way seems to have run along the Chilterns, skirted the Fens and entered Norfolk at Thetford, and may have had its origins in animal migratory routes across the North Sea Basin. There is no actual evidence for it beyond Ringstead, but it was a line of communication for centuries. The concept of a single track is doubtful, and it seems to have been a tangle of tracks heading in the same direction. How important it was, or if there were other routes, is unknown. One theory[15] is that it may have divided at Thetford, one branch fording the Little Ouse at Red Castle and continuing along the spur of higher land towards Hunstanton, the other crossing near Nuns Bridges and heading towards Norwich.

adopted and the traditional nomadic life of hunter/gatherers gradually abandoned. Near Hunstanton, identified plant remains include emmer (wheat), barley and hazel nuts, together with the remains of the bones of pigs, goats, cattle, red deer, wild cat and sheep, and the shells of mussels, oysters and cockles. Sickles, querns and pottery also appear, along with a wood henge monument (Arminghall, dating to about 2500BC), long barrows, a C-shaped enclosure (Broome Heath), a possible cursus earthwork (Beachamwell), and what might be dubbed Norfolk's first major industrial site (Grimes Graves). Now there was a much stronger bond between people and place. Trading over long distances was developed, and lines of communication opened up.

WATERY WAYS

Evidence of sea-going trade with Europe has turned up on both sides of the Channel, and one log boat, from St Albans, has been dated[17] to 4700BC. There has been much discussion on whether water/sea transport was less or more important, in economic terms, than land routes. Andrew Sherratt[18] argued that the 'Upper,' 'Lower' and 'East' Avon, with the Severn river, formed a water route which linked western Britain, including Wessex, with the South Coast and the Continent. He pointed out it was not then possible to sail up the East Coast of England as it was up the west, and that the Avon route may have been guarded by hill forts. Later, when materials began to be carried in bulk, the Thames was considered a more convenient point of entry to the country. But the whole question of water (rivers, The Channel, the North Sea) and land routes for haulage, and which was the most used, has been argued for a long time. On one point Sherratt was sure. 'This vision of prehistoric geography leaves no place for ridgeways, which are a modern ramblers' myth - it is high time that this romantic notion was pensioned off,' he wrote, arguing that it was riverine routes which provided the principal arteries in prehistory, and Celtic flat-bottomed boats which took advantage of it to provide maximum scope for an integrated riverine and maritime transport network.

BRONZE and IRON

Objects made of copper or bronze, such as daggers and axes, pins and awls, seem to have arrived in Norfolk about 2500BC, and local smiths subsequently developed high degrees of skill, as hundreds of bronze finds in the county testify. Then they added tools, weapons, ornaments, harness and dress fittings to their repertoire. Later still, and probably between 1200 and 800BC, gold also began to be used for fashion objects including necklaces and bracelets. East Anglia, of course, had no natural deposits of such materials, so much of it must have been obtained from traded ingots, artefacts manufactured elsewhere, or it was imported. Finds in

Norfolk so far also suggest there was a concentration of metal-making on the eastern edge of the Fens before about 1000BC. After that, the industry spread throughout the area. Bronze Age settlements are difficult to identify,[10] but it seems the population - largely in industrious farming communities - lived in small, circular timber huts with conical thatched roofs. The process of clearing areas of wildwood, which began in the Neolithic, was continued as arable farming and pasture became established. By now Norfolk presented a busy and increasingly open landscape of neat, ordered fields lined with hedgerows, in which raised barrows were visible landmarks.

The use of iron had been known in Europe since about 1000BC, but it was not until about 650BC that British smiths picked up the craft. Bronze continued to be used, but it was eventually sidelined because iron was harder and created a more reliable cutting edge. Iron Age people lived in a tribal society, the Iceni - which may have been a loose grouping of dispersed local communities - apparently populating Norfolk, north Suffolk and parts of Cambridgeshire. They lived in small round houses, heated by a central fire, in scattered and undefended farmsteads. They kept cattle and sheep, pigs and horses, and grew cereals, sometimes in areas cleared of woodland. Coppicing may have been another of their activities. Laid-out field systems may have been widespread, in which case Norfolk would have been a busy and enterprising agricultural area. It is clear they wasted very little. Broken or worn-out objects were usually repaired or put to other uses. They also built defended sites - notably at Holkham, Warham, South Creake, Narborough and Thetford - minted coinage, supported a warrior class which used light chariots, and produced gold torcs.[19] But this was, quite noticeably, the kingdom of the horse, which seems to have been held in particular esteem. There was some trading between neighbouring tribes, but from about 50BC a new commercial influence began to seep across the country when Roman traders, many using France as a springboard, began to make trading inroads into the British tribal territories. For some reason the Iceni stayed somewhat aloof from much of it, but it must have impinged on their consciousness. In any event the bustling countryside was now covered by an extensive network of farmsteads and fields, travellers and trade routes, roads and tracks.

THE ROMAN YEARS

In the years following the Claudian invasion of Britain in AD43, south-east England was slowly absorbed into the Roman Empire. In Norfolk, early military forts were established at Threxton, Ashill, Swanton Morley and Horstead,[10][19] and at least three principal roads constructed. These were the subsequently-named Pye Road, otherwise the modern A140; the Peddars Way;[19] and the Fen Causeway

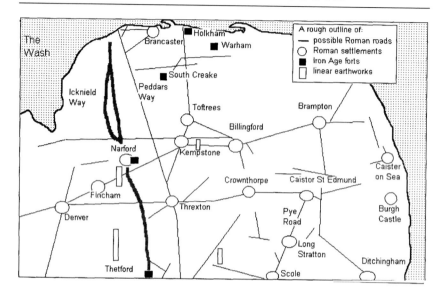

and its possible two branches, one of which (Watton and Crownthorpe to Caistor St Edmund) may have been the area's main west-east route, while the other traced a more northerly course through Castle Acre, North Elmham and Brampton. Whatever the actual sequence of construction, they seem to have been the skeleton of what became a diverse system of road communication.

With the new order came a new administration centre, Venta Icenorum (Caistor), which developed into a busy market town[26] and a centre for commerce and industry. Vessels moving upstream from the estuary to the east, the mouth of which extended from Burgh Castle to Caister on Sea, may have docked here. Smaller towns and villages, often at the nodal points of river crossings, crossroads or road junctions, were located at Denver, Fincham, Hockwold, Narford, Kempstone, Toftrees, Threxton, Brettenham, Billingford, Crownthorpe, Scole, Brampton and Ditchingham, among other places, each with their own trading catchment area. However, most of Norfolk's population, which probably numbered several hundred thousand, lived in villages or native-style farmsteads, providing the backbone of an economy based on agriculture and animal husbandry. In later years a cluster of wealthy landowners built villa estates in the area, some of them taking advantage of the spring line along the route of the old Icknield Way.

Road building methods varied according to what the road was to be used for, who was building it, what sort of terrain it was crossing, and what local materials were available. Many routes were simply farm tracks and village or homestead paths, which sprang up of their own volition or which had already been in existence for decades. Some were wide enough to allow two vehicles to pass, while one or two seem to have been laid out with military matters in mind.[16] These latter roads were presumably created by military surveyors in the first few years of the occupation when pacification and control were still top of the agenda. Later, as life under an occupying force became more bearable, and even welcome, road provision was able to take account of administrative and commercial needs.[26] The Peddars Way, for example, may have been built immediately following the Boudican rebellion of AD60/61 perhaps to modernise an existing trackway and to guard and facilitate the movement of troops and supplies arriving by sea.[19] The method of construction of major roads was essentially the same. Once the line was established the ground was cleared and drainage ditches dug on either side. Then soil from the ditches was piled in the centre and the configuration of the road built up by layers of flint, chalk or clay topped with rammed gravel. Overall, the Roman influence on Norfolk's communications network was immense. It was the first time the native population had experienced a planned programme of road construction and maintenance. The roads created a lasting impression, and it is nice to reflect that some still exist and are still in use today.

In Roman times some people travelled a great deal, walking, on horseback, or riding on a vehicle. Horses, mules and donkeys were used as pack animals, but it was clearly a very diverse transport system. For example, Raymond Chevallier[20] lists at least 18 different types of road vehicle, from a coal cart to a two-wheeled chaise and a four-wheeled cart used by the postal services. He also records weight restrictions - 200 to 600lb for light carts and 1000 to 1500lb for heavy carts - introduced to protect road surfaces. With people and animals constantly passing by, taverns and stables sprang up to

Roman stonework at Caistor St Edmund, near Norwich.

Studies of Anglo Saxon charters have provided a great deal of information about routes, and Oliver Rackham[50] has defined the following: the most important highways were called 'straet,' or street; 'herepath' evidently referred to highways wide enough to accommodate an army; 'weg' or 'way' was probably a less important route than a herepath; 'path' and 'stig' corresponded to present day footpaths and bridleways; 'hola weg' was a holloway; and 'lane' may have meant a minor road between hedges.

meet the needs of commercial travellers, muleteers, officials and vagabonds. Another important element was the cursus publicus, the Imperial postal system created by Augustus, which not only kept military men and administrators in touch with Rome, and facilitated the delivery of mail and official documents, but also helped to spread news. In the early days relays of runners were used, stopping at special stations positioned at intervals along the roads. Later, vehicles were used, which in turn demanded plentiful supplies of fresh horses, stabling, watering holes, places of refreshment and overnight stopping places. The average distance between overnight stages may have been between 18 and 23 miles, while relay stations on busy routes often employed a farrier, cartwrights, grooms, a veterinary surgeon and an administrative officer, who perhaps held the local franchise. The system was evidently efficient, official letters passing between Rome and London in a matter of days. Geoffrey Boumphrey[27] underlined the potential of the system by pointing out that London to Rome, for monied Romans, took 13 days, exactly the time taken in 1834 by Robert Peel when he was recalled to be Premier - and Peel, remember, was travelling post-haste, regardless of cost. In terms of private mail, Cicero[21] recorded that a letter sent from Britain by his brother, Quintus, on September 25 reached him on October 24. Some travellers used the extensive road system to see the world. Cato the Elder[20] travelled from Brindisi to Rome in five days, while Tiberius is said to have travelled 200 miles, from Pavia into Germany, in 24 hours. And a standard bearer, no doubt using relays of horses, once covered the 108 miles from Mainz to Cologne in 12 hours. There is also an account[21] of a journey from Vindolanda (on Hadrian's Wall) to York and back, which lasted from July 8 to 14 and which cost just under 95 denarii, some of it being spent on wine, barley, waggon axles, salt, fodder, wheat and lodging. And news of Nero's death was passed from Rome to Spain in six days. On the other hand, an army heavily laden with arms, supplies and booty could scarcely make five miles a day, while a legionary vanguard with pack animals and waggons might take two days to lumber 15 miles.

Life on the roads of the Empire must have been busy and colourful. Foodstuffs moving to town, wares being distributed from local workshops, traders, soldiers, waggons, merchants, layabouts and officials, all jostling for space. There were bridges and causeways, fords and stone inscription panels, milestones and rutted tracks, and in the towns, noisy, swarming crowds. There were sacred places and altars, too, set up beside the roads or by junctions, sanctuaries where travellers could find a moment of quiet to pay their respects to[20] Hercules, Mars or Mercury, or to the divinities attributed to the meeting places of two, three or four roads (Biviae, Triviae and Quadruviae). A certain Titus Irdas,[21] an auxiliary infantryman seconded to the Governor's Guard, even went to the expense of erecting an altar dedicated to 'the god who invented roads and pathways.' But of course, he was a walker.

GLORIOUS MUD

About 410AD Britain was abandoned by Honorius and the Roman elite and left to fend for itself. Social and commercial chaos, administrative breakdown, massive inflation and external threat all followed, destroying any stability that lingered. Many towns, including Caistor St Edmund, were already in decline, and within 100 years much of eastern England was in Anglo-Saxon hands. Ominously, the indigenous British population simply disappear from the pages of history. The early Germanic and Scandinavian invaders, including Saxons, Frisians, Jutes and Angles, undoubtedly brought bloodshed and confusion with them, but the archaeological silence of the British at this time constitutes an intriguing mystery. Nevertheless, by 500AD the East Angles of Norfolk and Suffolk had forged some sort of unity. Initially, Saxon populations were sparse,[25] though they were to grow rapidly. The peasants had simple lifestyles and homes made of timber and thatch grouped on isolated farms or in small, self-contained communities. Later, some of the settlements were linked by spiders' webs of tracks which may have begun life as driftways[16] for cattle, just as some village Back Lanes may have begun as animal tracks linking communities with their common pasture land.

Travelling conditions on pre-turnpike roads have always been a subject of dispute because records vary. King John's itinerant court moved on average 12 times a month[22] and sometimes managed 35, 40 or even 50 miles a day. And the Progresses of Elizabeth 1, including her trip to Norwich in 1578,[30] were little short of remarkable. But in 1586 William Harrison[22] claimed roads had deteriorated badly during the previous 20 years, perhaps because the Dissolution ended what little maintenance there had been and because they were under pressure from increased traffic. Conditions generally, particularly during wet and wintry periods, must have been awful. Yet William Worcestre,[23] a freelance clerical worker in Norwich, happily travelled from Norfolk to Cornwall in 1478, to Walsingham in 1479, and to Glastonbury in 1480. As for one Carey,[24] a professional courier, he awaited confirmation of the death of Queen Elizabeth 1, left London at 10am on a Thursday and arrived in Edinburgh with the news on Saturday evening. This after having been thrown by his horse and injured shortly after crossing the border.

Numerous writers have raised the possibility that wandering animals created the first tracks, including HV Morton. Sitting among the ruins of Ephesus,[29] looking at the marble bones of the old city and watching the shepherd-boys and their goats, he noticed that 'as the animals wandered here and there in search of grass and herbage, they trod winding paths which cut across the plan of the city. I have an idea that goats and sheep are the architects of the medieval lane!' The Greeks, Romans and Americans built their large settlements on rigid gridiron lines (witness New York, and Caistor St Edmund), whereas most native British cities sprang from more higgledy-piggledy beginnings.

Anglo-Saxon farming methods provide another explanation of why many of our country lanes contain unexplained twists and turns. The settlers tended to leave uncultivated strips (known as baulks) between the ploughed furlongs, initially to allow movement without damaging the crops.[28] Later, the strips became permanent tracks and then roads. Civil authorities used them to define boundaries, Church authorities to define ecclesiastical jurisdiction, and the clergy to assess tithes. So any subsequent attempt to realign them was suppressed at once. This led eventually to the annual ceremony of 'beating the bounds,' introduced to record and thus consecrate the parish boundaries. Procession Way, a stretch of the Peddars Way between North Pickenham and the A47 near Swaffham, is one example. As it was, only the Anglo-Saxon horse-borne nobility seem to have had the wealth or inclination to travel far, and those who did may have used the Peddars Way, the Pye Road and Stone Road (A144). Otherwise, little is known

about the main corridors of
communication. What is known is
that this was a hierarchical and
violent society governed by
noblemen and underpinned by
slavery. By the late 9th century
Thetford was one of the most
important local towns and ports,
with boats arriving up the Fenland
rivers from, among other places,
Stamford and St Neots.

Although the 10th and 11th
centuries did signal a somewhat
more prosperous time, the Danes
began intermittent raids on the
area which continued from about
800 until 1028, when Cnut became
king of England, Norway and
Denmark. At the time of
Domesday, Norfolk was much
influenced by water[31] -
watermills, freshwater fisheries,
salt pans, and water transport. In
the late 13th century Caen stone

*An old footpath between the village and
the church at Hackford, near Hingham.*

for Norwich Cathedral arrived at Yarmouth by sea to be loaded on to river boats for
the journey to Norwich. There were sheep in low-lying coastal areas and blocks of
woodland in the centre, while the best of the agricultural land was in the south,
between Norwich and the Suffolk border. Norwich, with about 5000 people, was
the largest community, though still rivalled by Thetford; Yarmouth was a fishing
village; and Castle Rising a salt producing area with access to the sea. But the
condition of the most important roads was declining, and would continue to decline
for a long time. Chevallier[20] thought one reason was the 12th century development
of the shoulder-collar, which gave scope to bigger vehicles with heavier loads, plus
the later invention of the pivoted front undercarriage, which allowed waggons to
make better use of tight bends. Thus the old Roman roads and Saxon tracks faced
the squeeze from a number of directions, rather as heavy lorries are damaging
and changing today's rural lanes. Another reason was an expanding economy and
the granting of charters for markets, which gave further impetus to the volume of
traffic. Because of their importance some of the roads were placed under the

king's protection, while the Statute of Winchester (1252/8) laid down that roads connecting market towns should be widened and vegetation cleared from the verges in order to aid visibility and foil miscreants. Other roads were also improved and bridges were built - often as pious acts - including examples at Stoke Ferry, Wiveton and Wroxham.[32]

The system seems to have been modestly successful. In March, 1256, Henry 111 was able to tour Norfolk in 11 days, calling at East Dereham, Castle Acre, Gayton, Walsingham, Thornage, Gimingham, Bromholm, St Benet's and Norwich. The weakness, as ever, was that there was no centrally planned roads strategy. All too often the network was the hapless victim of constant encroachment and local whim. It should also be remembered that medieval roads, in the main, were unlike Roman roads in that they were not physical entities with defined boundaries.[22] Rather, they were rights of way with legal and customary status. If a route was much frequented then it became a physical track, but a traveller still had the right to diverge if it became wet or obstructed, even if that entailed trampling on crops. On hills or banks, multiple tracks developed, so that travellers could choose the best. It was a reasonable enough system, but it may have nurtured the beginnings of traditional enmities between farmers and walkers.

During wet weather many of the roads became rivers of mud and water, and in winter some would have been impassable. In 1339 Parliament had to be postponed because so many people were held up by the conditions. Nevertheless, heavy loads were transported, by road and water, and sometimes roads maintenance was undertaken. Flint metalling repairs have been found on the sites of deserted medieval villages,[33] while the Church, in the shape of its abbeys, often took a hand in the upkeep of routes and bridges and the welfare of travellers. Those willing to help the programme with labour, gifts of money or bequests, were given religious indulgences and absolutions, while as an act of piety poor travellers were given free hospitality and helped on their way. The roads must have presented an extraordinary scene - minstrels, vagabonds, merchants, pilgrims, preachers, friars, collectors, horsemen, waggoners, messengers, justices, revenue collectors and pardoners - colourful, bawdy and squalid.

The number of travellers was to increase again, particularly in the years after the Black Death, when inflation and a shortage of labour persuaded landowners to convert arable land to grass and expand sheep farming. Many villages became extinct or were deserted, and large sections of the population had to search for shelter or better paid work. Other influences came into play, too. For example, the first coach in England[24] arrived from Holland to be presented to Elizabeth 1 in 1565. Pubs are said to have improved, too, with carpets replacing rushes, forks instead of fingers, music at meal-times and common dishes, into which all dipped,

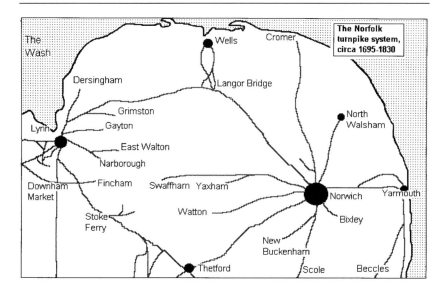

done away with. Yet it was a double-edged sword. The Reformation stopped the work of the abbeys in its tracks, bequests dried up, and no-one was held responsible for maintenance. Meanwhile, more and more people and vehicles poured on to the wretched roads. Of course, there were diversions. In 1547 the village of Foulsham,[32] having received money from the sale of church plate and vestments, used it to pay for repairs to two furlongs of drove used daily by the poor to drive their dairy cows to the common. But in general the road system was a squalid mess. It was holding economic growth in check.

TURNPIKES, ENCLOSURES and SURFACES
About 1600, the Thetford road to Bury St Edmunds was little more than a sandy track across a heath,[16] and even 150 years later there was very little change. The Thetford to Brandon way was also a notorious sandy waste, while the present B1145 between King's Lynn and Gayton was said to be the worst road in all England in winter. On the other hand, in 1675 John Ogilby[2] recorded gleefully that the Lynn to Norwich road was 'affording a very good Way, (much open and Healthy) as indeed the whole County generally does, which makes it reported that King James once pleasantly said He would have all Norfolk cut out into Roads, to supply the rest of the Kingdom.' So the news was both good and bad. The underlying problems, of course, included a lack of overall policy, few good surfaces

Most turnpike Acts came late to Norfolk, and most roads were never turnpiked at all. David Dymond[32] suggests that less than eight per cent of Norfolk's roads were thus improved, the majority remaining in their 'natural state.' Some landowners did improve non-turnpike roads, though this may have been to speed harvest produce to market or to reap the benefits of enclosure. Attleborough to Wymondham (1695) was Norfolk's first turnpike, followed in 1708 by Hethersett to Wymondham. The Thetford to Newmarket road was not completed until 1788. Most of the others centered on Norwich and Lynn, including: Norwich to Scole (1768), to Yarmouth via Ormesby (1769), Swaffham (1770), Watton (1770), New Buckenham (1772), Holt (1784), Aylsham (1794), North Walsham (1797), Cromer (1811), and Fakenham and Langor Bridge (1823); and Lynn to the Wash and Downham Market (1765), Narborough and Dersingham (1770), Wisbech (1786), Thetford (1792), and Fakenham (1828). In 1830 the causeway between Acle and Yarmouth was built.

and little regular maintenance. Then in 1663 a new Act provided for the repair of a highway in the counties of Hertford, Cambridge and Huntingdon (the Great North Road), and for the introduction of tolls. The second great age of road building was about to begin. The idea was that once Parliamentary approval had been enacted a local trust would be formed to look after sections of major routes, the money raised, and the roads improved. Expenditure, maintenance and the initial debt were to be serviced from income from the tolls. Once again, however, there was an element of short-terminism in that the trusts were established for only 21 years, after which it was assumed it would be well within the scope of the parishes to look after the roads. The word turnpike, incidentally, derives from the barrier, at first a pivoted bar which looked like a spear or pike. These were later replaced by sturdy gates and stone tollhouses. But the name stuck, and toll keepers became known as 'pikemen.'

Inevitably, the system was not universally popular. First, the barriers presented a challenge to anyone, traveller or drover, determined to avoid paying the dues. There were other problems, too. The turnpikes brought little immediate benefit to the parishes, some of the trustees were incompetent or dishonest, surcharges were added, and many of the pikes were continually in debt. Indeed, it seems likely that only a relatively small portion of toll income was actually used for road maintenance. Sometimes tempers spilled over, culminating in the Rebecca Riots of 1839/1844 which came about as a result of an excessive number of barriers being erected in impoverished areas of south-west Wales. Almost inevitably the destruction of a tollhouse was added to an already lengthy list of offences punishable by death. Nevertheless, unpopularity must not be allowed to obscure the fact that the trusts did greatly improve the country's main routes, turning a multiplicity of muddy tracks into a system of single routes.

Turnpikes came early to Norfolk in that £200 to improve the Attleborough to Wymondham section of the London road was offered by Sir Edwin Rich in 1675, though it was not acted upon for a further 20 years. Perhaps the surveyors were simply waiting for the draining of Attleborough Mere,[16] a major obstacle on the main Norwich/London route. In 1904 one writer[107] described pre-turnpike Attleborough as 'isolated on lonely flats,' surrounded by commons, and a place which 'must have been singularly aloof from the world.' Ogilby (1675), he said, had once described the 'Meer' as a cross between a bog and a lake which stretched on either side of the road. In Rich's time the road was 'unfenced the whole 29 miles between Thetford and Norwich, and plunged in the 14 miles between Larlingford and Wymondham into successive bogs and waterlogged flats … even now an oozy plain, but then a veritable piece of fenland.' Anyway, a year or two later the traveller/writer Celia Fiennes, on the same stretch of road, reported being stopped by 'a barr at which passengers pay a penny a horse.' A monument in a layby at Besthorpe commemorates Sir Edwin's benevolence. Thereafter matters slowed, the bulk of the final turnpike system in Norfolk having to wait until the 18th century. Then, two main clusters of roads used King's Lynn and Norwich as focal points, though a map of the county's routes does throw up some oddities. For example, there was no completely turnpiked link between Lynn to Norwich, but a gap between Narborough and Swaffham. However, the pikes to Fakenham and Langor Bridge did provide a continuous link. Again, there were connections for, among other places, Grimston, Gayton, Fincham, New Buckenham, Bixley, Yaxham, Downham Market, Wells, Thetford, Cromer, Yarmouth and Wisbech. The larger town links are explainable by commercial requirement, though some of the others seem to reflect little more than local wealth and influence, and thus the availability of capital.

According to Faden's map of Norfolk,[34] dated 1797, the county then boasted about 40 tollgates, though there were almost certainly many more. The tollhouse at Etling Green, near East Dereham, still stands. Some of the 1811 tolls for the Norwich-Cromer road included: coaches, 3d to 1s 3d (according to the number of horses); waggons, 3d to 8d; cattle, 8d per score; sheep and pigs, 4d per score. Arthur Cossons[102] pointed out that some of the vehicle restrictions (wheel width, wheel construction, lading weight, number of beasts of draught), later used to levy tolls, actually pre-dated the pikes. In essence, they represented belated attempts to try to protect road surfaces. For example, in 1654 no cart or waggon could be

A footbridge and ford near Walsingham.

drawn by five horses, or six oxen and one horse, except while moving loads of millstone or timber during the summer months. And in 1662 a lower limit of 6in was imposed on wheel width. Conversely, by 1755 broad wheels had to be cylindrical (upright), not conical (slanted), because whereas conical wheels ground the surfaces to pieces cylindrical wheels tended to consolidate them. He also pointed out that according to Norfolk's highways return of 1839 the county possessed, among other things, 349 miles of turnpike and 112 miles of paved streets or roads.

But the days of the pikemen were numbered, one reason being that improved surfaces greatly increased the speed and efficacy of traffic - by now the great age of coaching (see later, and Chapter 3, Making the Difference) had arrived - another that the coming of the railways rapidly siphoned off the passing trade. Many of the trusts went bankrupt. The last in Norfolk, the Wells and Fakenham, was dissolved in 1881. However, at least one fragment of the system survived until the mid-20th century. In 1954 it was reported[116] that Blanche Reeve of Syleham was the only tollkeeper left in East Anglia. She looked after the bridge over the river Waveney (the dividing line between Norfolk and Suffolk) which maintained contact with the villages of Stradbroke and Wingfield, in Suffolk, and collected fees (1d a wheel, cyclists 1d, walkers and local people free) which paid for the upkeep of two bridges and a small stretch of road. There was a white-painted tollgate, apparently, which was always kept closed except on Christmas Day.

Yet another major rural influence, the enclosing of common and waste land and the large scale re-organisation of agriculture, also changed communications and the landscape. Faden gave us a glimpse of Norfolk in the last years of the 18th century, when much of the county was still a maze of tracks linking isolated farms near heaths and commons, when the Hundred Stream still divided West Flegg from Happing, and the traveller from Caister on Sea to Happisburgh had little option but to follow the high water mark along the beach. But things were already on the move, and in the decades following publication of the Faden map they were to change irrevocably.

In all over 300 Parliamentary enclosures were enacted in Norfolk involving, during the 18th and 19th centuries, some 400,000 acres. In some cases enclosure was a tidying-up process following the abandonment of open field agriculture, or it brought small commons and waste land into production. In any event over 30 per cent of Norfolk was affected. The process was usually the same. Once Parliamentary approval was obtained Commissioners (inevitably drawn from the ranks of the nobility, the Church, minor gentry and landowners), a surveyor and valuer were appointed. After a survey and a period of public consultation, often involving acrimonious disputes, the Commissioners re-allocated the land in compact holdings and in what was supposed to be a fair and even-handed way. Internal field divisions were then

One of the most extraordinary of the English road builders was John Metcalf of Knaresborough (1717-1810), commonly known as Blind Jack. Metcalf is said to have become blind at the age of six, but he was a fine athlete and countryman. He was also a carrier, a fiddler, a moors guide and a horse dealer, who rode in several races. He once walked from Harrogate to London and back, and during the '45 Rebellion was a recruiting sergeant, being present at the battles of Falkirk and Culloden.

In 1754 he began a coach service between Knaresborough and York, and 11 years later won the contracts to make three miles of road between Harrogate and Boroughbridge. Perhaps with Roman road builders in mind, or perhaps copying the ideas of the French road builder, Tresaguet, who began improving roads at Limoges in 1764, he laid firm foundations, covered them with material which he arched to shed water, and dug drainage ditches on either side. He ultimately built or re-made about 180 miles of turnpike road. Metcalf is said[2] to have personally surveyed and laid out many of the roads he built, having a reputation for unerring accuracy.

amended and the holdings enclosed and encased in a framework of regularly shaped new roads. Scrub was cleared, heathland ploughed, woodland felled and marshes drained. Life for the poor was transformed. The effect, of course, was that the loss of common land caused widespread destitution, contributed substantially to rural depopulation, and drove the labouring classes into the hands of capitalism in the shape of urban industrialisation. It also produced the plaintive lament:

'His law locks up man or woman
Who feeds the goose from off the common,
But then it turns the villain loose
Who steals the common from the goose.'

Seven million acres of common land and fields[35] were affected between about 1700 and 1914, with a peak during the French Revolutionary and Napoleanic Wars, though there was a rapid decline in the number of Acts after 1865 when the American Civil War ended and the importation of Midwest foodstuffs to the UK began. This effectively removed the incentive to enclose common land for arable farming, and according to Friar[35] coincided with an increasing demand by the expanding urban population for open spaces for 'health and exercise.'

Norfolk's first Act for 'draining, improving and inclosing' a common at Stokesby was dated 1720. The last, for enclosing 47 acres of Saxlingham Common, came in 1863. A legacy remains, notably in areas of regularly patterned landscape, in the loss of heath and common land, and in roads built by enclosing surveyors. One example is the road running from the A11 to Spooner Row, as is the road from Spooner Row to New Buckenham. There are other examples in the Fens and even in Norwich, for the present Salhouse and South Walsham roads, which replaced sandy tracks across Mousehold, are enclosure roads built about 1820. An example of the effects of Parliamentary Enclosure was graphically illustrated by Tom Williamson,[36] using Before and After maps of Hickling. Prior to 1808 the higher ground around Hickling was surrounded by marsh and water, including Long Gores Marsh, Wiggs Broad, Colts Common, The Stub, and Hickling Heath. Following the 1808 enclosures, there were new field boundaries, drainage dykes and some new roads, while many of the marshes, including Wiggs Broad, disappeared.

Meanwhile, the provision of improved road surfaces gained impetus through the expertise of two Scotsmen, Thomas Telford (born 1757) and John Louden McAdam (born 1756). Telford, a child of industrial Britain, was a respected engineer. In 1803 he won his first major roads contract, earning himself the cheeky nickname 'the colossus of Roads.' He made his name as a road builder in the Highlands, his predecessor in that area being General Wade, who had engineered a network of military routes following the Jacobite Rebellion of '45. Telford went on to build canals and bridges and brought sound engineering principles to bear on roads, insisting on drainage, substantial foundations of stone blocks, and the use of graded stones which, he found, were crushed into a smooth surface by the iron shoes of horses and the iron tyres of waggons. After visiting America and Europe, McAdam was appointed a commissioner for highways in the 1780s, and in 1816 became highways inspector for the Bristol district. He was regularly consulted by turnpike trusts and became a household name. His system was also popular because it was cheaper than Telford's method. McAdam also used graded stones and gravel, but he dispensed with Telford's expensive foundations, believing that roads did not need unyielding bases of stone block but

Ambitious ivy, near Catfield.

substances which allowed themselves to be crushed and compacted to provide a smooth and almost waterproof surface. There were still problems, notably dust, but the transformation of England from an agricultural and mercantile nation into an industrial society would not have been possible without the development of an improved communications system.

As it turned out, the horse was to have one more grand fling before the advent of the engine finally sent it packing. This became known as the Golden Age of Coaching (see also Chapter 3, Making the Difference), which developed during the latter part of the 18th century thanks largely to these new road surfaces. Before it was finally driven into a corner it was to exert a profound influence on society. In 1754 the waggon journey time from London to Manchester[37] was four days. Thirty years later the time had been cut by half, while by 1830 some 54 passenger coaches per day were travelling in each direction on this one route alone. Six years later 700 mail and 3300 stage coaches operated regularly out of the country's major urban centres. The coaching phenomenon was a remarkable enterprise and it provided an opportunity for travel which had never existed before. In turn, it also spawned a massive support industry. Travellers needed warmth, refreshment, and a bed for the night; teams needed changing, horses shoeing and stabling; coaches servicing, loading and unloading. Town and wayside taverns and inns sprang up to handle this new trade, and a whole chunk of folklore - which in turn inspired countless Christmas card artists - came into being.

Imagine the scenes. A night mail sweeping through turnpike gates. The bustle of dawn departures, and accidents and overturnings on the road. Snowbound coaches and frozen, jolted passengers. Be-ribboned coachmen and sweating horses, post-boys and ostlers, guards and clerks, and inn yards, all bustle and smell and hooves clattering on the cobbles. Frozen harness and hurried meals. Boot boys shouting, horses champing, and the thrill of departure, at 10 to 12mph, aboard one of the flash new wonders of the highway: Telegraph, Union, Quicksilver, Regent, Highflyer, Tantivy, Comet, Rocket, Lightning, Hirondelle, Monarch, Expedition, The Times, Morning Star, Old Blue, Lord Nelson, Patriot, Regulator, Accommodation, Hope, Retaliator, Dart, Victoria, Norfolk Hero, Herald, East Anglian, Union, Griffin, or Express. Coaching bugles and drunks, races on the road, coachmen straining to be there first. Fallen trees, broken wheels, candle lamps flickering in the night. Coach travellers were the new elite, and so once again the foot traveller found himself at the far end of the queue[24] at the new, smart taverns. The coachmen were an elite,

In 1849 Mrs Amelia Bloomer, of New York, introduced her female walking costume, associated with the Women's Rights Movement[1] and a relatively new female interest in walking. The general fashion in those days was for voluminous skirts, which made it impossible to climb and uncomfortable to walk. It was taken for granted that skirts could not be abandoned, so Mrs Bloomer came up with the idea of a skirt - which ended a few inches below the knee - over Turkish trousers gathered in at the ankles. They were not popular.[105] The word bloomers, however, entered the popular vocabulary.

too. When William Salter, the Yarmouth stage coachman, died in 1776 aged 59 and was buried at Haddiscoe, part of his gravestone epitaph[16] read:

'... true to his business and his trust
Always punctual, always just
His horses could they speak would tell
They loved their good old master well
His uphill work is chiefly done
His Stage is ended, Race is run
One journey is remaining still,
To climb up Sion's holy hill ...'

THE ENGINE AGE

The invention of rail travel turned transport in this country on its head. Despite initial scepticism and fashionable jibes - 'tea-kettle,' 'potato-can,' and the problem of sparks damaging the ladies' clothes, not to mention setting trackside vegetation alight and frightening the horses - it soon made its presence felt. In the 1830s and 1840s it developed into what historians subsequently described as a 'mania.' Once the 'iron horse' had begun to flex its muscles everyone wanted to climb on board, for it was soon realised that one train could carry as many people as 30 mail coaches and more freight than 100 waggons. Financial backing flowed in - over 8000 miles[37] of track were built by 1855 - and passengers queued to try out this new power in the land. In one year, 1830, the Liverpool to Manchester railway, one of the first of the passenger carrying lines, transported 445,000[24] people (see Chapter 3, Making the Difference).

Collectively, the impact of the railway companies on the Victorian urban landscape was enormous. Now the landless and the rural

'The Motor Car Act of 1903 decreed that every vehicle should be registered, licensed, carry number plates, lamps, an audible warning device, and observe speed limits. A year later statistics showed that just over 17,800[27] vehicles of all types were registered, a figure which grew to 388,860 by 1913. In 1930 a new Road Traffic Act abolished the 20mph limit and brought in third party insurance, while five years later a new 30mph speed limit was introduced. That same year the number of people killed or injured in motor accidents was calculated to be over 230,000.

poor could travel to the cities to work among the new factories and industries. Steam also changed the rural outlook, for the building of the lines (signalling, levels, embankments, tunnels, cuttings, bridges, stations), sometimes by local labour but often by unruly gangs of itinerant labourers, represented the most extensive civil engineering programme the country had ever seen. It also changed the perception of travel; the railway was fast and exciting, but for the first time travellers were removed from reality, less aware of their immediate circumstances. If a mail coach stopped on the road the passengers, close to the windows and the coachman, immediately knew why. This was not the case with the train. Now they were isolated from the outside, their well-being in the hands of others, often unseen. But if the impact on the cities and the landscape was huge it was just as great on the existing road network. One of the first to feel the pinch was the coaching trade, which promptly died. By 1841 the mails were being carried by rail; by 1842 most of the stage coaches had gone out of service; and by 1850 many famous old inns had closed, their yards littered with the debris of rotting, discarded coaches. The glory of Tantivy and Hirondelle was to be seen no more, while the coachmen passed into folklore. For the turnpikes the impact was equally

*Lorry damage in Wicklewood,
pictured in 1997.*

devastating, and one by one the trusts were wound up or declared bankrupt. The effect was to force the country's main road routes into disrepair and return them to purely local use and a burden on the parishes. Once again maintenance was left largely in the hands of local roadside stone breakers while the main roads, which not long since had felt the flying hooves and wheels of the cross-country coaches, now supported merely 'the farmer's cart and the gentleman's carriage,'[38] and later, the horseless carriage.

Salvation for the crumbling roads, when it came, originated from a number of different sources, though the main thrust was public opinion. The Locomotive and Highways Act of 1865 set a speed limit for the new fangled road vehicles of 4mph in the country and 2mph in towns; one person had to steer the vehicle, a second had to stoke the engine, while a third was required to walk 60 yards ahead carrying a red flag. Much ridiculed, it was popularly known as the Red Flag Act and it remained on the statute books for 30 years. The reasoning behind it was that early warning of the presence of an engine on the road enabled horsemen to take evasive action before their animals bolted from sheer fright. Two years later, in 1869, another new contraption appeared on the road. It was promptly named Boneshaker, instantly perceived as a public menace, and duly became an object of derision. As with the steam train, however, matters took an unexpected course. For some reason the fashionable Mayfair and

A partially metalled lane over the old heath at Hackford, near Hingham.

Belgravia set took it up, larking about and parading themselves and their machines through Battersea Park.[24] The popularity of the bicycle was sealed. Soon there were improved models on the market to meet increasing demand. Whereas the Boneshaker had wooden wheels and iron tyres, the later Ordinary had a high seat and required a special costume while the Safety, which appeared in the 1880s, boasted rubber tyres and had the general appearance of the bike we know today. Very slowly, it was the cyclists who re-opened the roads and who - aided by pressure from the new and active Cyclists' Touring Club and the Cyclists' Union - began a campaign for improved surfaces. The 'cads on castors' suddenly became the great innovators, reviving the art of touring, revitalising the inns, re-opening the ale-houses, and inventing tea shops and bed and breakfast establishments. But the battle for popularity and better roads was long and hard. In the 1890s cyclists still had to walk long distances[38] to save their tyres from stones, and in May,

Any history of travel and
commercial life on the road
inevitably underlines a tradition
of continual 'improvement' in a
sense that speed constantly
quickens while the size of load
increases. An attempt at
comparison is open to all sorts
of interpretation, but here is my
tilt at an average miles per
hour chart:
Drover with cattle, one and a
quarter miles; heavy cart, one
and a half miles; packman with
animals, two miles; light cart,
three miles; walker, three miles
plus; carrier's cart, three to four
miles; bicycle, five miles plus;
stage coach, eight miles plus;
horse and rider, eight miles
plus; mail coach, 10 miles;
motor vehicle, 35 miles plus.

1897, a group of Norwich YMCA cyclists[39] was set upon by ruffians in Rackheath. One rider was pushed from his bicycle and injured.

Some historians are convinced it was cyclists, and the popularity of cycling, which rescued the roads network from the doldrums, though it has to be admitted that other influences were also at work. Steam trams and road steamers (buses), and even electric cabs and trams, made first tentative appearances. However, in 1888 Edward Butler introduced the first English petrol-driven engine capable of attachment to a moving vehicle,[37] and in 1895 Frederick Lanchester produced the first English four-wheeled car, while Herbert Austin designed a car ultimately built by the Wolseley Sheep Shearing Machine Company of Birmingham. That same year the Hon. Evelyn Ellis drove across England while deliberately ignoring the red flag requirement. The following year, 1896, the Red Flag Act was revoked. Though most horses and many people remained sceptical, the 'chattering stink-pot' had at least become lawful. A few months later, in January, 1897, Howes Brothers of Norwich[40] introduced a motor car, a Victoria, to the streets of the city to 'familiarise citizens and horses with the new form of transport.' A few days later a second vehicle was also introduced. Restricted to 16mph, and despite narrow streets and poor surfaces, the experiment was nevertheless deemed a success. Howes Brothers concluded, correctly as it turned out, 'there is a great future for this means of locomotion.' During the first decade of the century the motor car established itself, ultimately spawning the bus, the lorry and the char-a-banc, and eventually, telephone boxes, garages and petrol pumps,

AA patrolmen, guest houses, signposts, and a new travellers' taste for tea drinking.[24] In 80 years transport had passed from horse to steam to petrol, and by 1920 the highways were over-crowded again. But what of the roads?

The cyclists' pleas for better surfaces, now joined by the growls of the owners of petrol engines, did not fall on deaf ears. In 1870, following the demise of the turnpike trusts, a Highways and Locomotion Act decreed that all dis-turnpiked roads should be re-classified as main roads.[41] So far so good, but Norfolk Quarter Sessions

A footbridge at Knettishall.

smelled a rat in that some of the old turnpikes, particularly a cluster in the Stoke Ferry area, seemed to have served narrow, private interests, and in their eyes there was no case to allow them to become a burden on the rates. The Local Government Board was unmoved, however, and re-classification went ahead. Not until 1919 was the matter settled when the Stoke Ferry roads to Barton and Cockley Cley, East Winch to East Walton, and Roydon to Grimston, were the only 'main roads' in Norfolk not classified as 'main' by the new Ministry of Transport.

In 1889 the new Norfolk County Council inherited a network which included 823 miles of main roads and upwards of 300 bridges, many of which were crumbling or rotting, for some were made of timber. Matters were exacerbated by an increasing use of heavy traction engines and steam engines - in 1890 NCC bought its first steam roller, for £400, first using it on road repairs at Catton - and in 1898 the council had little option but to list 11 bridges for urgent repairs and ban heavy traffic from some others.[42] There was another unresolved problem, dust, which had dogged travelling since the age of coaching, forcing some passengers to wear goggles and some parishes to provide roadside pumps and regular road watering. The challenge was to find a substance which protected

The busy A11 near Attleborough.

surfaces from mud in winter and dust in summer, and experiments continued for many years. In 1902, in one bizarre trial, 2500 gallons of Texas oil were pumped by modified water cart on to the road between Farnborough and Aldershot.[38] Apparently the method had been used successfully in the United States, but the British climate proved too moist for it to work properly here. Five years later tar was tested, and a mixture of hot tar and chippings was eventually found to be the most effective. In 1903 new legislation decreed that all vehicles should be registered and licensed. Ten years later the number of vehicles legally on the roads[27] numbered 388,860. The petrol engine was an irresistible force, and within the next 15 years horse buses became extinct and most tramways came to the end of their economically viable life. Meanwhile, Norfolk County Council struggled to keep pace with the demand for road space. In 1910 it had 1400 miles of main road to protect, and in 1913[42] the highways department employed 700 men, many horses and three steam tractors, figures which were to fall dramatically during the First World War when labour was short, gravel (much of it from Belgium) scarce, the horses commandeered, and when troop movements repeatedly damaged road surfaces.

In the 1930s Ministry of Transport planners, looking for new ideas, began to cast their eyes at the Italian autostrade and the German autobahnen. These networks were very efficient and modern compared to England's meandering ways, but as Geoffrey Hindley pointed out,[43] both schemes were developed by militaristic regimes which obtained funding by blending social policy with military requirement. In 1930/31, NCC and the MoT finally agreed on the Norfolk's trunk road network, which is still essentially the same today. Several improvement schemes were proposed and then dropped through lack of money - a Wymondham bypass was first proposed in 1930, though London traffic continued to trundle through the Market Place until 1959 - but Norwich Ring Road, one of the first in the country, was built, in part deliberately,[10] to relieve local unemployment. During the Second World War roads across airfields and the Stanford Battle Area were closed, the Watton to Thetford road being one example; while the road between Tunstead and Scottow was dualled[10] apparently for the benefit of heavy lorry traffic to RAF Coltishall. Since 1945 the DoT has been responsible for trunk roads - with the NCC caring for the rest - at the same time giving Norfolk a relatively low priority. The first bypasses appeared in the 1950s/60s (King's Lynn being one of the first) and 1970s, which also saw changes to the Norwich-Lynn road which isolated Wendling, Honingham, Fransham and Necton, and later East Dereham and Swaffham, from the main A47. In the 1980s other bypasses changed patterns again among such communities as Attleborough, Thetford, Cringleford, Acle and Yarmouth West. Still without an inch of motorway, possibly the most Norfolk can look forward to in the near future would seem to be relatively small local improvements and the upgrading of sections of various main routes from single to dual carriageway.

Making the Difference

aving attempted in the previous chapter to construct some sort of skeleton outline of Norfolk's system of communications, I try in this section to put a little flesh on the bones. Subject matters have been chosen on the basis that they are of interest to, or are likely to be seen by, walkers. To confuse matters further, they are not in an alphabetical list (see Contents page for subject page numbers), but are placed in a spurious sort of historical order - earliest first and latest last - largely dictated by whim but a system which does at least place pilgrim routes higher up the list than Second World War tank traps. You will soon get used to it.

FORDS

One description of fords is that they represent points on the banks of rivers, streams or lakes where man or beast could cross with least difficulty. In reality, and next to where to find shelter, food and drink, the whereabouts of fords must have been one of the earliest lessons taught by parent to child. They were vitally important, acted as focal points for lines of communication, and helped fix the sites of many if not most riverine villages, towns and cities, including London, Thetford and Norwich. Fords were also unusually common, particularly in north-south travel in Norfolk, though in later years those on the most important routes were superseded by bridges. Today, in some places, ford and bridge can still be seen side by side.

Human ingenuity being what it is, attempts were sometimes made to improve crossing places by hardening the bed of the stream or river using stones or paving, though there is little evidence of it in Norfolk. One reason is that not a great deal of stone is available locally; another, that many fords must have been destroyed or greatly modified during the process of canalisation and the embanking of the rivers. Unbanked rivers in their free state would have wandered back and forth over their flood plains, and thus the sites of fords, or rather, the best crossing places, must also have moved over the centuries. There is a faint suggestion[45] that the Romans might have tried to 'stagger' the alignment of the Peddars Way, at least at the crossings of the Thet and Nar, in order to spread the load of crossing

The ford at South Acre.

traffic to reduce, as far as possible, the deterioration of river beds. The Romans are known[20] to have positioned places of worship at prominent features including fords, while in Gaul columns to a horseman god were erected near crossing places. In Broadland, the waterways provided the arteries of communications, and according to Tom Williamson[36] early in the Middle Ages a series of fords were established at key points which included Ludham, Potter Heigham, Wroxham, Weybridge (near Acle) and Wayford Bridge. The last two names, derived from the Old English waeg, even suggest pre-Conquest

The word ford is surprisingly common among place-names, suggesting that fords were common, while Eilert Ekwall[44] pointed out that 'when a village grew up at a ford it was named from the ford.' In Norfolk, Lenwade, Shernbourne (Weybourne), and Carbrooke (Brooke) are also suggestive of crossing places, while a glance at a map reveals many '-ford' names, perhaps the best known being Thetford.

origins for these crossing points. Several hundred years later Faden's 18th century map[34] largely ignores fords, perhaps because they were too common to list and would have cluttered his charts, or because, even by 1797, many fords must have disappeared and been replaced by bridges. However, he does mention two at the southern end of the Peddars Way (Blackwater and Droveway fords; now canalised, both of which had thick, black mud bottoms in the 1970s), and another at Forncett Common, near Wacton Magna. Alas, there was no mention of it on the OS map sheet of 1886.

Fords have left their stamp on history and social history, in place-names in which the element 'ford' is still common (I counted 22 on one Norfolk map); in folklore (for example, references abound in literature and art); in an occasional dot on a map (current Ordnance Survey Landranger charts mark surprisingly few, for most have been piped, embanked, or bulldozed away); and in the occasional surviving ford, such as South Acre, though even here it has been tamed by hard surface approaches and a bridge for foot traffic. You can often see clues to the former presence of a ford as you drive or walk through a number of Norfolk villages. Signs proclaiming, 'Liable to Flooding,' or warning, 'Test your brakes,' often mean that here was a ford which once in a while attempts to reclaim its former glory.

STONES and LEYLINES

With little suitable local stone available in Norfolk other than flint, it follows that most large visible lumps tend to be ploughed-out pieces of flint, glacial erratics, or imported puddingstone (conglomerate), sometimes shaped, used for grinding corn, and then later discarded. Very often such stones were used as mounting blocks or as corner posts to protect walls and buildings from passing vehicles; yet large stones do, for some reason, generate disproportionate volumes of myth, speculation and disagreement. One example is the Cowell Stone, near Swaffham, which stands where the Roman Fen causeway crossed the Icknield Way and which has been the subject of a great deal of speculation. Its name[16] may derive from the Saxon word 'doule,' meaning boundary mark, or from the name Growell, known in nearby Beachamwell in the 13th century. Ben Ripper,[46] however, said the stone was 'allegedly' named after Cow Hill and marked the parish boundaries of Swaffham, Marham and Narborough; or it might have been a corruption of coal and stone, perhaps being placed to guide travellers to a beacon hill, possibly near Colkirk. Some even maintain it had mystical properties, or at least a sufficiently important influence to persuade Roman surveyors to use it as an alignment for the Fen causeway; others, that it was dragged to the crossroads at some later date. Current thinking is that it is a glacial boulder, possibly set up in Roman times.

Some of the blame for the kerfuffle can be laid at the door of Alfred Watkins who deduced the existence of straight sections of track[47] at all periods, from the prehistoric to the medieval, from the apparent fact of alignments, or 'sighting points,' and who published some of his theories in The Old Straight Track in 1925. As a result, the later cult of leylines was to bury itself deeply into the psyche. Taken to the extreme it is a confusing and perhaps misleading path to follow, because although there is no doubt that landscape landmarks must have been used as navigational aids, just as later on church towers and beacons were also used, the fact remains that early tracks were not straight but wandered according to whim and circumstance. Yet even Geoffrey Boumphrey,[27] as late as 1939, was writing about the 'simple savage' of the Old Stone Age setting up his markstones across treeless landscapes of 'immense vistas,' of surveyors invested with 'magical powers,' and of stones invested with sacredness. It has been difficult to shake off the legacy. Perhaps there is a grain of truth somewhere amid the myths and markers, for overland journeys were certainly undertaken throughout the Neolithic, Mesolithic, Bronze and Iron Ages, and descriptions and directions must have been handed on somehow. But the leyline theory is an idea too far for most archaeologists, for four basic reasons: statistical probability (maps invariably reveal alignments of some sort, but there is little rhyme or reason in them and many seem mere coincidence); time scale (linked sites are often from different eras, even different centuries); improbability (many leylines would seem to serve no apparent

The Cowell Stone, near Swaffham.

purpose); and pattern (how do you impose leylines on the known pattern of history)? The best and most thorough examination of this cult subject is by Tom Williamson and Liz Bellamy.[48] Their conclusions are worth reading.

Large stones can still be seen dumped at the side of fields to reduce the chance of damage to ploughs, or used as gate post supports; while glacial erratics are particularly prolific in the Aylsham area because of the sequence of geological deposits. But the curiosity remains. As Alan Davison[49] pointed out, 'Only when surface stones are of unusual size or weird shape do they attract attention and are, perhaps, put on one side as objects of curiosity.' Some early Anglo Saxon charters suggest stones were sometimes used as boundary markers if physical features (brook, marsh, wood, spring, old road, tree, dyke, etc) were not present. One mentioned in 1739 was the so-called Oxfoot stone of South Lopham, which formed the basis of several legends, though it seems likely it has been moved several times and may even have been used for a spell as a mounting block. A relatively modern example of marker stones are parish boundary stones, two of which, on the line of the Peddars Way between the rivers Little Ouse and the Thet, survive to this day.

BARROWS
Aside from the Iron Age forts at Holkham, Warham, South Creake, Narborough, Thetford, and a possible sixth at Tasburgh, some of the most visible of pre-Roman man's marks on the Norfolk landscape are barrows. The Neolithic period in Norfolk left an enclosure (Broome), a wood henge (Arminghall, dated to about 2500BC), at least four long barrows (West Rudham, Broome, Harpley and Felthorpe), a large industrial-sized flint mining site (Weeting), and a possible cursus near Beachamwell. Cursus, incidentally, are enigmatic constructions of long, parallel banks with outside ditches which can be anything up to six miles long. Their original use is not known, though suggestions include processional ways, race tracks, funeral games, astronomical functions, and tribal territory markers. It is the Bronze Age which seems to have left the largest legacy, for the traces or actual remains of upwards of 1500[11] round barrows from this period have been logged in the county, including some at Little Cressingham, Salthouse and Weasenham All Saints. Looking at a sites map they seem to cluster in particular on both sides of the later Peddars Way, around the later site of Norwich, and towards the North Norfolk coast, though this interpretation may be misleading as many barrows have undoubtedly been destroyed by ploughing, particularly on the heavier, clay soils. Barrows must have been very visible landmarks in an often wide open landscape. The people buried beneath them, presumably the social or political elite, were invariably placed there with a variety of pots, weapons or, in

rare cases, jewellery. Best
known to many walkers,
perhaps, are the Bronze Age
barrows visible from the
Peddars Way near Anmer and
Houghton Hall.

HIGHS and HOLLOWS

A natural inclination to
keep one's feet dry led to
the early development of
the causeway, common in
the Fens and the Broads,
which involved either the
laying of a toughened
surface over the boggy bits
- as timber and branches
were used in the Somerset
Levels - or the physical
raising up of a road by
the building of an
embankment. In the Fens

*A parish boundary marker on the
Peddars Way near Rushford.*

the Romans also made use of levees, though on peat they employed oak trunks
with branches and stones and metalled the surfaces with wattle, gravel or gypsum.
Sometimes they also seem to have raised up their roads in the vicinity of rivers, or
flood plains, as they did with the Peddars Way at Thorpe Farm, near Thetford.
Some say this raising up of roads led to the descriptive and familiar name, High
Street. A causeway was once the main means of access to the Iron Age fort at
Holkham, which stood in a sea marsh, while Wormegay, once a low 'island' in
the Fens, was joined to higher ground in the west by a similar raised road. In 1896
a massive timber causeway, 100 yards long, was discovered in Norwich[61] linking
higher ground on either side of the river near Fye Bridge. Originally assumed to
be of Roman date, it was later thought to have a Saxon origin. In the Middle Ages
many wet routes were improved, and Dymond[32] says causeways certainly existed
by the 13th century at places like Setchey, Fakenham 'Dam' and Haddiscoe, this
latter link being a sinuous two-mile track over the Waveney marshes. Wey Bridge,
which once connected Acle to the island of Flegg, had a bridge by 1101, though
an earlier stone causeway is said to lie upstream. There are also references to a
causeway at Newland, near the Tuesday Market, King's Lynn, which approached

the ford and ferry across the Ouse; while a causeway from Horning Upper Street, later cut by modifications to the course of river Ant, once led to St Benet's Abbey. Another causeway ran north from the abbey towards Ludham, crossing the Hundred Stream. More modern causeways, dating from the 1830s, include The Straight from Acle to Yarmouth and the old raised bank of the A17, now disused, from Sutton Bridge to Cross Keys across the former Wash estuary. Other ancient causeways have been supplanted by modern roads. One of the best known in the country - Maud Heath's Causey, near Chippenham in Wiltshire - was built as an act of charity. Maud was a pedlar who all her working life had to carry her wares from Bremhill to Chippenham market across the waterlogged Avon flood plain. When she died in 1474 she endowed the building and maintenance of a four-mile causeway, from Wick Hill to Chippenham, built in part on a series of brick arches.

Holloways tend to occur on inclines where traffic has struggled up and down, perhaps for centuries. Over the years the action of rain water, hooves and wheels leach away the unpaved surface and cut a groove into the side of the hill. Oliver Rackham,[50] in perhaps the best book about the countryside, says well-developed examples can take 300 years to form. They are certainly a feature of some deserted villages where former streets can be identified running between house platforms and crofts. Mary Hesse[51] has written of a possible Roman road between Barwick and Egmere/Waterden, known as Holgate, which became a deeply sunk lane in places and was probably at least 300 years old in 1250. Holloways are not particularly common in Norfolk but some lanes and green lanes, mainly on gentle inclines, still display an inclination to drop between shallow banks to a surface lower than the surrounding land. In most cases modern road metalling has arrested their development.

BANKS and DITCHES

The line of sea walls which can be traced around the edge of the Wash, and commonly called Roman Bank, are more likely to have been erected during the 7th to 9th centuries. David Dymond[32] pointed out that the place-names Walton, Walpole and Walsoken suggest that local communities invested heavily in sea defensive work at the time, one example being the byroad between Walpole St Andrew and Cross Keys, which was raised up. Defensive work in the peat Fens was also undertaken during the 17th century, and in the Lynn Wash area from the 18th through to the 20th century. Defensive work, including sea banks, has been undertaken on the Norfolk coastline for centuries. The best preserved of the county's linear earthworks exist, or can be traced, in the west and south of the county and include Fossditch, Bichamditch (Beachamwell), the Laundith, the Panworth Ditch, and the Devil's Ditch (at Garboldisham). In the main they were lines of banks and ditches seemingly designed to cut off chunks of countryside with otherwise natural boundaries (valleys, marshland) and to block lines of communication. The Launditch may have been created in the Iron Age, but the rest seem to date from the AD400 to 550 period, and seem to reflect the confused conditions of the 5th century when Anglo Saxon immigrants were in conflict with native British groups struggling to maintain their independence. The earthworks cross at least three Roman roads and one prehistoric droveway.

Church ruins at Tunstall.

EARLY FARMING

Farming seems to pre-date settlements, for there is evidence from elsewhere that Mesolithic communities may have indulged in cereal growing to supplement their hunter/gatherer economy. In Norfolk the earliest clues tend to come from the Neolithic period. Traces of plant remains at Spong Hill (North Elmham) and Broome Heath (Ditchingham) point to the growing of einkorn wheat and barley and the collection of hazelnuts and crab apples. Later Neolithic remains from Redgate Hill, Hunstanton (emmer, bread-type wheat, barley) and Grimes Graves (acorns, etc) suggest that wild plant food remained important for a long time. Bones from Redgate Hill indicate the presence of domestic pigs, cattle, goats, possibly sheep, and occasionally roe and red deer and even wild cat and dolphin, with the shells of mussels, oysters and cockles. Later deposits at Grimes Graves indicate cattle, sheep, pigs, deer and horses. The landscape was extensively cleared during the Bronze Age, and by the Late Iron Age there is evidence of spelt wheat, hulled barley, emmer, and grain storage pits.

EARLY CHRISTIANITY

Christianity began to spread in the 1st century AD and reached Britain by the 3rd century. Initially, its adherents were to be found mainly in the urbanised towns and cities, but the emperor Constantine's acceptance of Christianity as the official state religion, in 312AD, ensured that much of Roman Britain was Christian before the end of Imperial rule a hundred years later. One early Christian symbol was the chi-rho - the first two letters of the Greek word Christos - sometimes accompanied by the letters alpha and omega. Other symbols included vine, fish, dolphin, peacock, pomegranate, doves, palm fronds, the Tree of Life, and a sacred vessel, the cantharus. The cross was evidently not generally employed until after AD600. Christian finds from the Roman period include lead tanks (Icklingham, Suffolk), liturgical vessels and equipment, and pewter or silver plate and vessels (Mildenhall, Suffolk). Early buildings[54] tended to be urban basilicas, rural churches, and house or estate churches.

The beliefs of the early Christians were at variance with those of their forebears. A single deity was to be worshipped, private property was held in little account, high moral standards were set, and sacrifices forbidden. Nevertheless, the Church slowly and deliberately absorbed some of the pagan rite and symbolism. Even so, paganism continued to survive and in 597 a papal mission sent by Gregory 1 and led by Augustine landed in Kent. Within months, Christianity was adopted by the king, Ethelbert. But there was another problem. Augustine's model was a long way removed from the form of Celtic Christianity which had flourished far from Rome in isolated, scattered monasteries and missions. In 603 Augustine attempted to close the gap, without much success, but within 30 years most of the north was converted. Meanwhile Raedwald, the most powerful East Anglian ruler, was baptised in 616, while his son, Sigbert, sent St Felix to East Anglia and gave the Irish monk, Fursey, a site for a monastery at Burgh Castle. After Sigbert's death the throne passed to Anna, whose daughters Etheldreda and Withberga established several abbeys, including Ely and East Dereham. In 664 the Synod of Whitby finally resolved the differences between the two British Christian models and a 'national' church was established which transcended geographical, political and military divisions. Indeed, by 680 it was so well established in East Anglia it was decided to divide the see, and by 803 the northern see (the north folk, Norfolk, as opposed to the south folk, Suffolk) had been established, most probably at North Elmham. Information about the Church in the region during the 8th century is sketchy, perhaps because many records were destroyed during later Danish incursions, but it is known[55] that books and scholars were resident in the area. There was also an enormous programme of re-building after the Conquest, and the prosperity of early medieval Norfolk, reflected in its countryside and expanding towns, gradually took more permanent form in the shape of many magnificent new churches.

Local 5th and 6th century church buildings were presumably constructed of timber, and have vanished, for the earliest stone churches appear to be no earlier than AD700. Tradition has it that Norfolk's first church was built by Felix at Babingley, close to the former small port of Castle Rising, some time after AD631, but there is no hard evidence to support this. Nor is there much evidence to support some of the early ideas (Saxon defensive towers, bell towers, a lack of suitable stone to build corners, etc) about round tower churches, of which the county has over 120. More recent research[10] suggests many of them were built during the Romanesque period between the 11th and 12th centuries and that they seem to echo an architectural fashion of similar buildings in Schleswig-Holstein, north Germany, suggesting cultural links during the early Middle Ages with countries bordering the Baltic and the North Sea.

The ancient bridge at Wiveton.

During the last 1000 years more than 1000 parish churches[56] were built in the county, for at least 928 certainly existed between the 11th and 16th centuries. Some 620 of them are still in use today. By the 13th century there were also over 1000 English monasteries, while the sites of over 150 religious houses are known in Norfolk, as well as 'hospitals' and colleges of canons. The first Benedictine

Walkers crossing The Mermaid stream near Brampton.

monastery in the county was St Benet's abbey, founded by king Cnut in 1016. The first Cluniac house in Norfolk was founded at Castle Acre, with other important centres at Thetford and Bromholm. Much later, the Reformation brought fundamental doctrinal and liturgical changes, and continued upheavals in religious affairs in England and elsewhere, which finally led to the formation of a number of nonconformist sects including Independents, Baptists, Quakers and Presbyterians.

BRIDGES

The Romans certainly built bridges, sometimes with stone piers and timber superstructures, and sometimes timber, though most had probably decayed by the time of the Conquest. In any event there are few traces of Roman bridges in Norfolk - there was little or no stone, and timber tends to rot - save at Downham West[16] on the Fen Causeway, and possibly at Threxton. Bridges were expensive to build and costly to maintain, and in general there was a very slow transition from fords to timber bridges and then to stone bridges. The medieval attitude seems to have been mixed, for while some notables and parochial authorities were reluctant to bear the cost, other guilds, fraternities and notables did subscribe to the ideal, and many bridges built were associated with religious foundations or chantries. By 1300 Norwich[53] had five bridges over the river Wensum, and there were also bridges at Trowse, Harford, Earlham and Cringleford, an unusually large number which seems to reflect the importance of the city as a commercial, religious and administrative centre.

Many early medieval bridges were simple stone structures, wide enough to accommodate packhorses and their panniers, though later designs were wider and supported by piers and arches. Sometimes there was a ford alongside for waggons to use. Occasionally the bridges incorporated abutments, or refuges, into which travellers could press themselves to avoid passing traffic, and cut-waters, triangular wedges of masonry to divide the current and protect against erosion. The Common Law of England required that the bridge builder was also responsible for the cost of the upkeep, and thus they often provoked acrimonious disputes, usually over maintenance and boundaries, which were sometimes in the middle of the stream or river concerned. Occasionally tolls were charged, or special taxes (pontages) raised towards the cost of upkeep. Many bridges were built as pious works, the original St Olave's bridge being one example. Wiveton bridge, at the head of the old maritime estuary, is a late medieval survivor, while an unusual bridge in the grounds of Walsingham Priory (see Packhorse Trails) may be Norfolk's only known example of a packhorse bridge. In Norwich, Whitefriars[53] is said to be the site of the earliest bridge over the Wensum, perhaps dating from 1106, while Bishop Bridge, the only surviving medieval bridge in the city, is one of the oldest in the country, albeit in restricted use. There were earlier bridges on the site, which also marks the line of a former Roman road, but the one you see today was built between 1337/41. It is not entirely typical because it was originally erected as part of the city defences and once had an arched gatehouse. Many of the city's bridges were improved in the early part of the 19th century, while Foundry Bridge and the old City Station bridge owe their existence to the railways.

HUNDREDS and PARISHES

The Hundred administrative unit may have evolved following the English re-conquest of the area from the Danes, for Domesday listed 33 in Norfolk, by which time they were clearly well established as areas of administration and taxation. In fact they remained as sub-units of local government until 1834 when they were replaced by the Poor Law Unions. Although contours changed over the years, some Hundreds used rivers or even Roman roads as boundaries, while some Hundred meeting places seem to have been at fords (Mitford, Eynsford), beside crosses (Brothercross, Guiltcross), or near hills or mounds, recognised by the words 'how' or 'hoe' (Carleton Forehoe). Parishes may date from the 9th or 10th centuries and some could relate primarily to economic rather than ecclesiastical needs, even though most parishes had at least one church. Though the smallest unit of administration, some are of great antiquity while others may have emerged because of boundary changes or settlement disappearances. Some of the boundaries were amended and simplified in the 1920s.

MARKETS and FAIRS

Markets and fairs are very old, and it is at least possible the first in Britain were held within the earthworks of Neolithic causewayed enclosures. Certainly during the Bronze and Iron Ages there were sites for bartering and exchange at strategic places, such as cross-roads, while in Roman towns the central paved forum - as at Venta Icenorum, the 'market-place of the Iceni' - provided space for trade. Gradually there developed the tradition that whereas markets were held at regular places on regular dates, fairs were perhaps twice-yearly seasonal events, sometimes held on saints' days. At these, farmers brought cattle, peasants their produce, people from remote hamlets walked in to obtain their stocks of goods and clothes for the year, news was exchanged and entertainments enjoyed. Unsurprisingly, buyers, sellers and trinkets salesmen flooded in. Fairs were big events on rustic calendars, one reason being, as Thomas Burke[24] pointed out, that few people travelled purely for pleasure, the bulk of traffic being related to manufacture and trade.

The Normans laid out planned developments at Norwich (moving the old Saxon market from Tombland to its present site, closer to the castle), Castle Acre, Castle Rising and New Buckenham, but between the mid-12th to the mid-14th centuries markets appeared all over Norfolk, constituting a major commercial revolution. According to David Dymond[32] there is evidence for at least 138 medieval markets in the county, an unusually high

The Norfolk Hundred administrative areas were: Freebridge Marshland, Clackclose, King's Lynn, Freebridge Lynn, Grimshoe, North Greenhoe, South Greenhoe, Docking, Smithdon, Brothercross, Gallow, Launditch, Wayland, Shropham, Guiltcross, Diss, Depwade, Forehoe, Mitford, Eynesford, Holt, North Erpingham, South Erpingham, Tunstead, Happing, Taverham, West Flegg, East Flegg, Great Yarmouth, South Walsham, Norwich, Blofield, Henstead, Loddon, Earsham, and Claveringham.

density. Market charters proliferated and in some cases (including Thorpe Market, Downham Market, Burnham Market) helped shape local settlements. But it should be remembered that a charter date does not necessarily date the origin of a market, for many were in existence long before charters were granted. Even so, it is possible to say that whereas Norwich, Thetford and Yarmouth had Anglo Saxon markets, charters suggest other origins at places such as Holt, by 1086, Lynn 1100, Upwell 1203, Burnham Market 1209, Acle 1253, Elsing 1380, East Harling 1475, and so on. In many cases the sites were marked by a market cross.

Not all markets were successful. They were very competitive and the siting and the spacing between them was critical. Sometimes the spacing, often determined by a manorial lord with a degree of trial and error, was clearly wrong, and some struggled and failed. Also, fewer charters were granted after the Black Death of 1349 until by the 17th century only 31 places[10] were rated in Norfolk as market towns. Population decline, better transport systems, and a rise in commercial specialisation, had all played a part.

DEER PARKS

Fallow deer, introduced by the Normans, were more numerous than red deer in medieval Norfolk, and venison was an important part of upper class diet. No royal forests are known in Norfolk, but at least five[10] chases (open areas devoted to hunting deer and other animals) have been located, the most important being Rising Chase. Some deer parks - of which over 90 sites are known in Norfolk - were enclosed by hedges, ditches or oak pales, and a few (Wymondham, Thornage, Mileham, Old Buckenham, for example) are still traceable in hedgerows and field boundaries. Some local sites were presumably established before 1200, the last as late as the 16th and 17th centuries, and they varied in size from 60 acres (Pulham) and 80 acres (Winfarthing) to 310 acres (Shelfanger) and 500 acres (Whinburgh).

PACKHORSE TRAILS

Some evidence for packhorse routes emanates from the 10th century, but the system may be even older than this. They were a common sight from the 14th to the 18th centuries, being the articulated lorries of their day and the main method of hauling large quantities of goods over long distances on unmetalled routes largely inaccessible to wheeled transport. What is more, there is also evidence[2] that perishable goods such as china, glass and mirrors were carried this way, rather than by waggon, coach or chaise, because of the packing skills of the packmen and the sure footedness of the animals. As the use of packhorse 'trains' proliferated so improvements were made to aid their passage. Between 1650 and 1800 many packhorse bridges were built, usually sufficiently wide to take one animal at a time and with low parapets so that loaded panniers were not disturbed. Some tracks were metalled, causeways were built in very wet areas, and elaborate gradients developed in hilly country.

Ponies, often sure-footed Galloways, and sometimes donkeys, were used to carry coal, charcoal, salt, wool, stone, cloth, ironstone, fish, barley, oats, malt and other goods in trains sometimes 40 animals long. Such trains would have a lead horse wearing a bell collar to warn other travellers and trains of their approach, and an accompaniment of four to six men. In this way a Galloway could carry a 2cwt load for eight hours, while larger horses could carry 6cwt. Given good conditions they could cover upwards of 20 to 25 miles a day.[52] In turn, animals and men required water, stabling, shelter, food, and beds for the night. The provision of these services helps to explain inn names such as The Packsaddle, The Packhorse and Talbot (a talbot being a train master's favourite dog), and the Woolpack. Fairs and markets, ports, monastic estates, overseas trade, and the growth of industrial practices, all helped to boost the volume of goods hauled by packhorse and in key parts of the country, with pack trains passing continuously, they must have been a frequent and exciting sight. The decline of the system seems to have begun in the 18th century as road surfaces began to improve and the use of waggons for haulage became more economic. The development of the railways dealt the ponies a final blow, though some freelance packmen lingered until the First World War.

In Norfolk, there is no evidence of any particular road or bridge being provided specifically for the use of packhorses, one possible exception being a somewhat unusual bridge in the grounds of Walsingham Priory. But there is no doubt pack animals were a common sight in the area, being used extensively by Norfolk's larger ports to move cargoes, and by commerce and industry to move goods.

PILGRIMS

Pilgrimages seem to have sprung from the 4th century acceptance of cults of saints and the veneration of relics, and they became a remarkable preoccupation, stretching across Britain and Europe to the Holy Land. Two of the main centres in England were Canterbury (Kent) and Walsingham (Norfolk), where the original shrine stood for 500 years until it was destroyed in the 16th century. Norfolk also boasted a second attraction, Bromholm or Broomholm, near Bacton, a small Cluniac community established in 1113, which was revitalised in 1223 when it obtained what were claimed to be two pieces of the True Cross. Miracles were announced and pilgrims flooded in. Alas, the relics disappeared in 1537 when they were being sent to London, whereupon Bromholm went into steep decline. Walsingham was hugely important, rivalling Canterbury in stature. Henry 111 is said to have made at least eleven pilgrimages to Norfolk[58] between 1226 and 1272, and Edward 1 made at least a dozen. Indeed, the 'waie from Walsingham to London' was listed as one of the 20 most important thoroughfares[57] of Elizabethan England, while the Milky Way, which was said to point across the heavens towards England's Nazareth, was re-named by many the Walsingham Way.

Holy wells were also frequently visited places, and some early place-names contain the element wylla,[12] meaning spring or well, such as Bawdeswell and Ashwell

The old pilgrim road, near Weeting.

(now Ashwellthorpe). There were springs at East Dereham, one dedicated to St Withburga still being in existence, and wells associated with churches at Wereham, Bawburgh (St Walstan), Costessey, Gressenhall, Burnham Norton, Taverham and East Rudham. The place-name Shadwell is a corruption of St Chad's well.

Few roads sprang from a single purpose, and there are no known roads used exclusively by pilgrims. One of the best known routes is the Pilgrims' Way[3] between Winchester and Canterbury, which by and large was the only route available, but in Norfolk pilgrims seem to have converged from all directions using stretches of Roman road and medieval tracks. Whatmore[57] mentions four main streams, from Norwich (through Hempton), from Upwell (through Pentney, West Acre and Massingham), and from Lynn (via Coxford and North Elmham). The other, of course, was from London. This route took the faithful and their co-travellers through Tottenham, Ware, Barkway, Babraham, Newmarket, over Brandon ferry, Weeting (by the cross at Mount Ephraim), Hilborough (where there was a chapel), North Pickenham (hermitage; using a short stretch of the Peddars Way, from Pickenham Wade to Procession Lane), Litcham (chapel and hermitage), Fakenham (crossing the Wensum by a ford slightly to the west of the town), Hempton, East Barsham and Houghton St Giles (slipper chapel). The way from London to Walsingham was undoubtedly the most important and, as on other routes, directional and spiritual comfort was provided by stones and crosses. Dymond[32] says that mid-15th century pilgrims would have passed five wayside crosses in the parish of North Elmham alone. Examples still survive at Aylmerton, Langley and Pentney, while the last time I saw the Mount Ephraim cross, in the 1970s, it was but a short stump. Support services for pious travellers also sprang up in the shape of inns, chapels of ease and hospitals, which looked after the poor and the passing pilgrims. The Hospitallers cared for the sick and protected the

The much-eroded and deteriorating pilgrim cross near Aylmerton.

pilgrims. Red Mount at King's Lynn was a pilgrim chapel, while one 'hospital' was provided at Billingford[55] on the Norwich road to Walsingham. Apart from pilgrims there were other people treading the same roads, too, including palmers - 'professional' pilgrims who begged their way around and collected shrine souvenirs as proof of piety - and pardoners, who sold indulgence certificates. Altogether, they added an extraordinary vibrancy to the roads. Incidentally, the word tawdry, meaning cheap and of poor quality, is a corruption of St Audrey's Lace which was sold at the fair of St Audrey (Etheldreda), queen of Northumberland and patron saint of Ely.

INNS and TAVERNS

First things first: a pub and a tavern are essentially the same thing, providing bars and drinking areas, while an inn is a small hotel. They first seem to have emerged during the Roman period when they often used a bush, a vine, a garland or a hoop to advertise their presence. By 1393[59] Richard 11, concerned as to the proliferation of such houses and the competition between publicans who brewed their own beer, decreed they should all display a distinctive sign. This is largely how pub names and signs, many of them now obscure, came into being and why some of them grew larger and larger. At least two signs in the region were so large they spanned the main road, in both cases the present A140. One was The Magpie at Little Stonham, the other The White Hart at Scole. Over-road signs, and even over-large 'gallows' signs, were eventually deemed dangerous to coaches and passing riders, and the practice was either curbed or the signs fell to pieces. By and large the first post-Roman inns were run by monks in the Middle Ages to serve all travellers, particularly passing pilgrims. Suddenly freed by the Reformation from the responsibility of preaching to travellers, and the mortification of the flesh, the inns of England gradually forged ahead of Europe in terms of comfort and style, peaking during the Coaching Age (see later) and during Victoria's reign. Even so, the traveller needed to proceed with caution. Dickens' Mr Pickwick sent Sam Weller on ahead to Towcester to

A roadside cross near Hanworth.

Norfolk dialect is becoming harder to hear, and traditional markets such as Swaffham and Norwich often represent the best chance, along with quiet country pubs. Here is a brief selection of dialect:[64] beck, stream; carnser, causeway; deeke, bank; drift, lane; flag, turf; fleet, shallow; foreigner, a stranger; harnser, heron; heater, where two roads meet; heater-piece, land in angle of two roads; holl, wide ditch; ligger, lifting lever or eel line; lode, artificial channel; loke, lane; lows, boggy place; pightle, small field enclosed by hedges; pit-hole, pond; rud, road; smur, heavy drizzle; staithe, landing stage; troshing, threshing. Ligger can also mean a plank over a stream, while No-Where, a place-name in six or seven locations, refers to left-over land. Staying with words, agger means the raised foundations of a Roman road, while levees and roddon (or rodham) are the silted beds of extinct rivers where the surrounding land level has dropped, leaving them standing proud like causeways. Another Fen word is smeeth, a series of unenclosed commons. Still near water, hythe is a wharf, while a haven is a sheltered place for shipping.

check the standard of accommodation. Caution was certainly necessary in the 15th century. William Worcestre, who worked in Norwich, began a journey to St Michael's Mount, Cornwall, in 1478, and described the clientele[23] at his first overnight stop. They included a tinker, a rabbit-catcher, a fiddler, a priest and his mistress, a seamstress, a ropemaker and a whore. 'Sleeping arrangements were sorted out amid puddles of vomit and cheap wine,' he recorded. This, I should add, was at the Piers Plowman pub at Thetford.

FERRIES

Few ferries remain in Norfolk, but ferry services do have a long history, certainly dating to Roman if not pre-Roman times. One oft-quoted but I think doubtful[19] example is a Roman ferry service running from the Peddars Way across the Wash to the Lincolnshire coast. In more recent times flat-bottomed barges were used, either rowed or hauled by a continuous chain or rope, capable of carrying passengers and sometimes light vehicles or pack animals. Local ferries such as those at West Lynn, Brandon and Stoke Ferry must have been widespread at one time. Tom Williamson,[36] writing of Broadland, says ferries tended to develop where rivers were too wide or too deep to ford, and that in the 19th century there were examples at Surlingham, Buckenham, Reedham, Brundall, Horning, Stokesby and Martham. The Lower Yare ferry between Yarmouth and Gorleston, which had a claimed history going back to Norman times, folded in 1997, but Reedham ferry still operates as a passenger and vehicle carrier. Services also operated in Norwich and

there is a reference[53] to
ferries, including Piggins'
ferry, near the Dolphin
Bridge. Perhaps the best
known was Pull's, Poole's
or Sandling's ferry, which
plied the Wensum between
Riverside Road and the
Cathedral Watergate and
which was once the only
public connection - use of
Bishop Bridge being
severely restricted -
between Thorpe and the
city. John Pull[60] was
appointed in 1796. He lived
in the Ferryhouse (now
Pull's Ferry), once part of
the Cathedral Watergate,

A cattle pound of 1830 near North Elmham.

which he also kept as a pub, changing his name to Poole at the same time. He died
in 1841, when the service was taken on by Mr Feltham, then Mr Harrison, and
finally Mr Mollett, who saw it close in 1943.

FORTS, CASTLES and MOATS
No castles were built in Norfolk until after the Conquest, but Iron Age forts
certainly existed at Holkham, Warham (the best preserved and most atmospheric),
South Creake, Narborough and Thetford, the first four of which seem to form a
defensive arc around an area of north-west Norfolk. Another earthwork at Tasburgh
may belong to the same period, or it may have medieval origins. During the late
Roman phase forts were also built at Brancaster, Burgh Castle (another impressive
ruin) and Caister on Sea.[26] The building of castles was largely introduced by the
Normans, though William's only East Anglian castle was in Norwich. Even so,
post-Conquest castles large and small included[10] Castle Rising, Middleton,
Wormegay, Weeting, Thetford, Castle Acre, Mileham, Old and New Buckenham,
Denton, North Elmham, Horsford, Norwich and Burgh Castle, with other possible
sites at King's Lynn, Quidenham, Wymondham (Moot Hill), Raveningham,
Yarmouth and Hunworth. Another category of late medieval constructions which
includes maisons fortes, or fortified manor houses, seems to indicate sites at
Martham, Oxburgh, Claxton, Caister, Wood Norton, Baconsfield and Gresham.

Moats present something of a conundrum, for they are a fairly familiar sight in the Norfolk landscape although few of them, it seems, were built for defensive purposes. Indeed, over 400 are known to have existed in Norfolk during the medieval period, a majority being constructed between the 13th and 14th centuries. About 70 per cent seem to be within the boulder clay region, with scatterings of others west and east. Most, but not all, once surrounded agricultural buildings or a dwelling house. Their purpose is not entirely clear and many suggestions have been put forward including clay extraction, water storage for fire-fighting, fish ponds, drainage, and pounds for stock. Another explanation, entirely plausible, is that they were simply a fashion fad which echoed the defensive moats of the castles.

MARITIME TRADE

Lynn and Yarmouth dominate any history of Norfolk's shipping and sea-going trade, but they do not tell the whole story. Both flourished after the Conquest and very slowly supplanted river ports such as Norwich as their positions at the mouths of extensive river systems enabled them to serve local areas as well as growing as sea-going centres. Lynn's foreign trade was already in existence by 1204,[10] while from at least the 12th century Yarmouth's fortunes were founded on the herring. In the 14th century Yarmouth also handled most of England's worsted exports. Between 1300 and 1350 its merchant fleet possibly comprised 60 to 100 vessels of 100 tons, plus many smaller vessels. In the 15th century Lynn attempted to arrest its decline by establishing trade links with Iceland, without great success, while Yarmouth lost much of its herring trade to the Low Countries. In addition, Yarmouth harbour began to silt up. Lynn had to wait until the 16th century before it was able to enjoy a fresh revival based on coastal traffic in coal from Newcastle. Many of Norfolk's lesser coastal communities operated as small ports and harbours, the most important being the Blakeney Haven complex of Blakeney and Snitterley, Wiveton and Cley,[62] although by the late 16th century Blakeney was also facing competition from Wells. The silting of channels and the coming of railways changed the pattern of trade yet again for areas in which smuggling had also had a part to play.

NAMES

The subject of place-names (and road and field names for that matter) is a thoroughly complicated business and you can cull far more information from Rye,[63] the Norfolk Atlas,[10] and Williamson.[12] In general terms the two most common Norfolk suffixes are -ham (village, estate) and -tun (farm, settlement). The latter, which suggests smaller places, has a general spread while the former seems to have preferred the better drained soils and river valleys and generally suggests larger places (such as Aylsham and Wymondham). Ham also tends to be associated with early personal names or topographical terms (ie, Burnham, river village), while ton/tun is often related to later personal names or some economic function (ie, Appleton, where apples were grown). Names ending -wick, -stead and -worth, like -tun, may have been subsidiary settlements which became  separate estates in the late Anglo-Saxon period, while areas suggesting woodland are sometimes indicated by -leah (or -ley), -holt and -wald. The ending -field means open country, implying that adjacent areas may have been wooded. A Scandinavian influence is also seen in -thorp, meaning a small hamlet (a word apparently borrowed by later English speakers) and particularly in -by. This suffix tends to cluster on the old isle of Flegg, suggesting 9th century Danish settlement.

Nordvico, dating to about 900AD, is the earliest known reference to Norwich,[65] while the river name Wensum seems to be derived from Waendsum, an Old English word meaning 'winding.' Some of the city's street names from 1300-1500 are known,[61] including Over Westwik (currently St Benedict's), Vicus de Nedham (St Stephen's), Berstrette (Ber Street), Holmestrete (Bishop's Gate), Hatter's Row (Guildhall Hill), Vicus de Swyne Market (All Saints Green) and Horsmarket (Rampant Horse Street). Research in rural areas, or more particularly Ashill,[66] has also thrown up some interesting road and track names, including the 14th century Marketgate (leading to Watton) and Holmereslane (leading to the pond); Rollescrossweye (to Saham Toney), which became Rolcrosfalgateway in the 16th century; and Randolfes Way (to Great Cressingham), which was evidently tidied into Reynolds Way in 1785. In the same village some 15th to 18th century names also seem to have described their nature: Brodgate (broad); Higate (on a ridge), which later became Hole Wey then Holloway; Greengate Way; and Burywey (to

Bury St Edmunds), later called Walsingham Way. Many fascinating names remain in the county. Some, like Crown Lane and Anchor Lane, were often associated with pubs, but within a short radius of where I live there are Dark Lane, Stepping Block Hill, Swingey Lane, Stone Brigg, Stonegate, Cake Street, Rattee's Corner, Policeman's Loke, and so on. The subject is worth several books on its own.

MAPS and SURVEYORS
The word map derives from the Latin mappa, meaning napkin, and although some of the first in Britain were produced as early as 1250 the first detailed county maps did not put in an appearance until the late 16th century. Christopher Saxton produced a series of English and Welsh counties in an atlas of 1579, while William Camden published his Britannia in 1607. Then John Speed (1542-1629) published a popular 'pocket' atlas. Cartography improved towards the end of the 17th century, notably through the work of Robert Morden and John Ogilby, whose Britannia of 1675 contained 100 plates of road maps printed in strips. Ogilby also invented a machine to measure each statute mile. By the mid-18th century details of local topography was available to wealthy visitors from abroad, and Charles Roberts[68] has written of a set of stage coach routes published in Paris in 1759 for French gentlemen travelling in England. Bound in soft leather and folded into two to fit a greatcoat pocket, it gave the London-to-Norwich distance, through 'Windham' and 'Heterset,' as 108 miles. Now kept at a chateau in southern Normandy, the routes are thought to be copies of the work of John Senex of Fleet Street (1719), who in turn had taken over the work from Ogilby. However, as far as Norfolk was concerned a more significant production was that by William Faden, geographer to George 111, who published a map of the county in 1797. Faden's team of surveyors, including Thomas Donald and Thomas Milne, worked in the county from 1790 until 1794, and the sheets themselves[34] were three years in preparation. There is little doubt that Faden's production has proved invaluable to historians, as it portrays the county on the brink of change prior to the parliamentary enclosures.

It was a threat of invasion from France in the late 18th century which produced a military requirement for good maps of the South Coast, and the job was given to the Board of Ordnance which hitherto had been largely responsible for artillery. The resulting one-inch per mile maps proved very popular. In Norfolk, the Board encountered particular difficulties with triangulation[67] because of a scarcity of high places, but thanks to diligent work by Capt Colby, Charles Bugden, Col Mudge, Lt Charles Bailey and many others, some of whom may even have been in the county at the same time as Faden's surveyors, various printings of Norfolk were made from about 1838 through to 1890, the latter being a composite which included the railway revisions. A national one-inch series was not completed until

1873, though a network of 20,000 'trigometrical stations' (trig points) - some set on elevated positions, as at Shepherd's Bush on the Peddars Way, or on tall buildings, often churches - was built up. Now disused, they enabled surveyors to measure angles and distances. Over the years estate and enclosure maps have also provided a great deal of information to researchers. The work of the old Board, of course, was eventually taken over by the Ordnance Survey. A patch of ground known as Surveyors' Land, where the surveyors are thought to have stored their material, still survives in Winfarthing. Now farmed, the rent goes to the parish council.

A very individual milestone at Blicking.

MILESTONES, SIGNPOSTS and STILES

The Romans erected at least 100 milestones in Britain, though few remain in situ and none have been identified in Norfolk. There are one or two clues, though, including a 1588 reference[16] to a 'Rome Stone' at Grimston and another documented possibility near Threxton. If the county did have any, perhaps they were made of wood and long since rotted away. The first post-Roman stones were erected on the Dover to Canterbury road in 1633, but these were specifically to regulate the cost of hiring post horses. The oldest surviving series of milestones were provided in 1728 by Trinity College, Cambridge, on the present A10.[35] Mid-18th century Acts made provision for milestones on all turnpiked roads, and some are still in place. Initially, some of the trusts vied with each other to produce attractive designs, employing local craftsmen who sometimes lapsed into the vernacular or abbreviated place-names and used Latin numerals, which confused visitors and made the stones difficult to read from passing coaches. About 300 milestones[69] of various dates remain in Norfolk, some having survived precautionary war-time removals in 1940. Many stones collected from within the city boundaries were destroyed in 1942 when a council depot in Heigham Street was bombed. Carol Haines[69] believes an evolution of styles is discernible, right through to when Norfolk County Council erected many more early in the 20th century. Some are of particular interest. A series at Blickling dates from 1796, while Outwell has a cast-iron stone complete with cross keys emblem which was made in Bradford for the local turnpike. Thursford has a modern example made by the Capps' iron foundry, which is also a family memorial. Another milestone/memorial, which stands on the Green at Acle, gives distances to Yarmouth by the old turnpike (1768) and the new Acle Straight (1831). The oldest in Norfolk is possibly the Holt Obelisk, thought to be a gatepost from Melton Constable Hall and given to the town in the 1750s. A similar gatepost given to East Dereham was destroyed in 1946. Norfolk also has a number of stones bearing the legend 'London 100 miles.' There are examples in East Dereham market place and near the Bridewell in Wymondham. There is another in Milestone Lane, Wicklewood, about 300 yards from where I live, which begs another question: why should an apparently minor route through an apparently minor village be graced with milestones? The answer is most probably the Kimberley estate. I assume Wicklewood's Milestone Lane and Church Lane lie on the route travellers to Kimberley would have used after branching off the Norwich-London road at Attleborough.

In one sense milestones and signposts are one and the same thing, but with the subtle difference that signposts were set higher to provide an improved visual aid to drivers and passengers using fast-moving wheeled transport. The earliest seem to have been erected by public spirited individuals in the 1670s, and although they were a legal requirement at most crossways by 1697 their development seems to have been sporadic until they were made a compulsory requirement in 1773. Many of the old finger-posts at crossroads have now been replaced by EEC-approved models.

Stiles (the word evidently comes from the Old English 'stigel,' meaning 'to climb') were originally designed to allow people, but not livestock, to climb over or through fences, hedges or walls, but over the years there has been a subtle change in usage. Many farm fields now include fences and stiles in areas where there are public rights of way, but no livestock. So they are also being used to channel walkers into a particular area or towards a particular route. Stiles can also magically turn into obstacles, or hurdles, particularly towards the end of a tiring day when leaden feet resolutely decline to clear the top bar. They can also be deceptive. Some small white-painted stiles, most usually seen near field boundaries, are possibly not stiles at all, but pipeline markers. One stile enthusiast is David Hasted of Harrogate[108] who evidently possesses a photographic collection of over 300 different models. The oldest he has recorded, at Foyle in Hampshire, evidently dates to the 17th century.

HEATHS and COMMONS
Before the enclosures huge acreages of commons, heaths, warrens, fens, moors and greens existed all over Norfolk. Thetford and Wymondham, for example, were all but surrounded by them. In 1796 Nathaniel Kent totted up the county's grand total as being somewhere in the region of 200,000 acres,[10] some of the commons having boundaries dating to the 16th century or, as in the case of Hales Green, the 14th century. Most were the ancient remains of areas of open land, or 'wastes,' associated with or even pre-dating the manorial system which underpinned medieval economic life. Faden's map[34] demonstrates how farms and cottages were often conveniently located at the edges. For centuries the commons provided fuel (wood, furze, turf), clay sand or gravel (building work, road repairs), recreation (fairs; and camping, an early form of football), grazing (sheep, cattle, horses), building materials (sedge, reed), and food (fish, eel, wild birds). Many parishes, such as Mattishall, also had greens (small commons), while Attleborough could boast Ling Common, Burgh Green, Cow Common, Swangey (swan island) Fen, West Carr Common and Oak Common. Long Stratton, on the other hand, had a Wood Green which (like Oak Common) may have evolved from primary woodland. One of the largest heaths was not, as might be expected, in Breckland, but north of Norwich. Mousehold once stretched to 6000 acres, and even as late as Faden (1797) it spread from Kett's Hill to Salhouse. Nearly 30 years after Faden's publication, when Bryant published his map, most of the open areas had gone.

AGRICULTURAL IMPROVERS
Norfolk's best managed estate in the 18th century was undoubtedly Holkham, for Thomas Coke, later Earl of Leicester, and despite a busy Parliamentary career, took a close interest in agriculture. In 1776 he began his annual sheep-shearings which developed into big occasions and in a sense foreshadowed modern County Shows. He improved the quality of local sheep by introducing the Southdown, and from 1790 onwards instituted continuous farming improvements. Others were also interested, including Lord Townshend at Raynham, and wealthy owner-occupiers in north-east England, and with a close eye on parallel developments in

Holland they began to tackle a range of problems such as poor soil fertility, a lack of animal fodder, fertilisers, crop quality and even farm design, improvements which reached a zenith in the mid-19th century when they were halted by an agricultural depression.

GREAT ESTATES

Because land bestowed status in pre-industrial society it had been possible since the Tudors to buy one's way into the landed gentry. From the 16th century the best form of investment was to buy an estate, and such was the amount of industrial age 'new money' being made in the 18th and 19th centuries that by 1880 half of Norfolk was owned by landowners with more than 1000 acres each. They ranged from gentlemen farmers to those with up to 50 farms on the rent roll. Some of them were estates of very long standing, for the Le Strange name had been at Hunstanton since 1200, and De Grey at Merton since 1306. Much of East Norfolk remained out of estates control, the area thus retaining its medieval houses and barns, whereas on the big estates farmsteads were replaced, farm houses and villages re-built, churches restored and schools built.

By the late 19th century the largest estate in Norfolk was Holkham (the Coke family) with 43,000 acres; followed by Raynham (Townshend) and Houghton (Walpole) with 15,000 to 18,000 acres; Melton Constable (Astley), Wolterton (Walpole), Marlingford and Bylaugh (Evans-Lombe), 12,000 to 14,000 acres; with Stow Bardolph (Hare), Gunton (Harbord), Merton (De Grey), West Acre (Hammond) and Kimberley (Wodehouse) in the 10,000 to 12,000 category. The landowners' most popular pastime was field sports, the preservation of game becoming an important ingredient of estates life. By the end of the century shooting alone sustained some of them, particularly those on poorer soils. In Breckland, a great deal of tree and hedge planting was undertaken to help sustain the game and improve the shooting, and many of the shelter belts and lines of gnarled Scots pines which give the Brecks their distinctive atmosphere date from this period. Between the wars, when many farms struggled to survive, large blocks of marginal Breckland was sold to the Forestry Commission for tree planting.

WILDLIFE

About 20 per cent of Norfolk's mammal species are thought to have been introduced, either deliberately or accidently. Even the domestic cat and the house mouse are immigrants, and not even the humble rabbit is thought to be native. As for that most Norfolk of dishes, the pheasant, it has Oriental origins even though it has been known in Britain since before 1058. Other introductions include Canada geese, edible frogs, Chinese water deer, muntjac, red, roe and Sika deer and even fallow deer. The Romans may have been responsible for fallow deer, and for the edible frogs, but many of the rest emanate from sources which include ships, pet shops, landowners, zoos and estates. An American rodent, the coypu, became fashionable for nutria fur in 1929, but by 1940 most of the nutria farms had closed and many of the animals had escaped. Starting in the 1960s it took over 20 years to eradicate them, the last one, allegedly, being killed in 1988. More modern reported escapees from zoos and wildlife parks include capybara, racoon, a leopard, wallabies, and a 'puma-like' creature evidently still on the loose.

THE COACHING AGE
The coaching age is deeply embedded in the national psyche - witness 'traditional' Christmas cards - and while there certainly was a bustle, charm, clamour and excitement about it, coaching was also dismally uncomfortable and occasionally dangerous. Steep hills (particularly difficult before brakes were invented), ice and snow, ruts, over-turnings, and vagabonds and ruffians were but some of the discomforts erstwhile travellers occasionally experienced. In the second half of the 17th century the earliest stage coaches, effectively larger versions of private town coaches, were plying between some of the more important communities, but a century later scores of them were competing with the mail coaches for passengers, changing patterns of travel, encouraging some towns such as Swaffham to develop, and rejuvenating the tavern trade. Some of the old coaching inns, with their arched yard entrances and fender stones, still survive. At their zenith in the 1830s, some 22 inns and taverns were mentioned by Dickens[28] in Pickwick Papers.

Mail coaches, four-wheeled covered vehicles designed by John Palmer of Bath in 1784, were adapted to carry the Royal Mail. Drawn by teams of four in seven to 10-mile stages, they first went into service[35] between London and Bristol, though the delivery system, which radiated out of the capital, had reached Yarmouth and most other places by 1807. By 1837 Norfolk's main mail routes[102] were: London (via Ely, Downham Market, Lynn, Hunstanton) to Wells; London (via Newmarket, Bury St Edmunds, Thetford, Wymondham) to Norwich; London (via Ipswich, Scole) to Norwich; and London (via Ipswich, Lowestoft) to Yarmouth. In addition, David Kennett's[109] list of ordinary (ie, non-mail) service routes included Fakenham to Barton Mills, Yarmouth to Bury, Norwich (via Swaffham and Lynn) to Spalding (Lincolnshire), and Lynn to Peterborough. The services were efficient and the mailmen generally dutiful, diligent and courageous. The London to Falmouth run, for example, covered the 176 miles in 16 hours and was said to be so regularly precise that clocks were set at its passing. Average speeds point to continual improvements. In 1811[102] the London/Norwich run was completed a 7.49mph, a figure which had improved to 9.01mph some 26 years later. Many of the Royal

Private Norwich-London coaches were running as early as 1665[70] - the Confatharrat ran to Bishopgate Street in 1696 - but regular services probably did not start until the 1760s. By 1782 there were at least four daily London services. After 1785, Lynn to Norwich was a seven-hour trip. Competition was fierce, but what began as reckless racing ended with owners stressing reliability and safety. During the winter of 1807 the Newmarket and Expedition coaches did not get through, the Bury coach overturned, and sometimes guards had to set off through the snow carrying the mailbags. The 1820s and 1830s saw a big expansion. Norwich to London was 13 hours; there were four services a day for Lynn, and 10 a day from the Norfolk Hotel (Norwich) alone, including the Royal Mail to Birmingham. Coaches brought Norwich news of victory at Waterloo (1815), and in 1814 driver Coldwell received the Freedom of Norwich. Other feted drivers were Thorogood (The Times), Joseph Wiggins (Phenomena), John Osborne (Yarmouth), and William Laws (The Telegraph). In 1844 the Norwich-Yarmouth railway opened and by 1845 most of the coaches had been scrapped.

Mail's later coaches were built by John Vidler of Millbank and painted scarlet, maroon and black. The guards, in scarlet uniforms, carried a blunderbuss, pistols and a horn. Once established, of course, the mail stages began to compete with private coaches for the booming trade in passenger traffic. Fares on the stage coaches were cheaper but they were not so comfortable as the mails, nor so well protected, which meant they were also more prone to attack. Nevertheless, by about 1800 the stage and mail coaches provided the main means of travel for a majority of the population.

One of the most successful of the coaching entrepreneurs was William Chaplin.[28] Between 1800 and 1825 he worked from five London yards, provided horses for half the London mails for the first stage out and the last in, and at one time had 60 coaches, 1300 horses and 2000 employees. His main competitor was a Mr Sherman, proprietor of the Shrewsbury Wonder, who shrewdly operated from the Bull's Mouth yard opposite London's General Post Office. That it was a punishing profession was noted by the diarist Joseph Farrington,[71] who recorded that 'the greatest number of those confined there (in the London Bedlam) were women in love, and the next greatest class was Hackney & Stage Coachmen, because of the effect on the pineal gland of constant shaking they are subject to.' Two examples of coach journeys will do. On the morning of April 13, 1775, Parson James Woodforde[72] left London for Norwich. He and his fellow passengers changed chaises at the Stagg, Epping, at Harlow and Stanstead; changed again at Bourne Bridge, Newmarket and Barton Mills; then travelled through

Thetford and Attleborough, arriving at Norwich after 10pm to find the city gates shut. Eventually they got through to the King's Head in the Market Place and were abed by 2am. He was not dismayed. 'From London to Norwich 109 miles, and the best roads I ever travelled on,' he noted. On January 5, 1803, and in order to attend James's funeral at Weston Longville, William Woodforde left Castle Cary in the Taunton coach[2] at 1.30pm, arriving in London at 1pm the following day. He left London by mail coach the same evening and arrived in Norwich on January 7, travelling on to Weston which he reached at 4pm. This journey represented 238 miles in just over 50 hours, 'without one minute's sleep.' Some 30 or 40 years later the Golden Age was over, the railways consigning the coachmen to oblivion, the horses to the knackers' yards and the coaches to rotting heaps of junk.

GALLOWS, GIBBETS and GRAVES
Highwaymen, footpads and ruffians infested the lonely heaths, hedgerows and byways for many decades, adding further concerns to the already hazardous business of travel. However, few of them seem to have lived up to much of the romantic nonsense subsequently written about them, though it is true some enjoyed a popular notoriety and that condemned highwaymen were sometimes visited in their cells by members of society. So bad did the security situation become at one point that the Post Office[27] advised the sending of all bank notes and bills in two halves and at different times, though in fact much of the impact of the footpads was lost in 1797 following a new Act which allowed money, meaning gold, to be carried in less easily realised forms such as notes and bills. Nevertheless, the names of a few of the breed have been handed down, including[24] Captain Maclean (the Gentleman Highwayman); the swaggering Jack Rann, who held a party with seven girls in his execution cell; Claude du Vall; James Whitney; and of course, William Nevison and Dick Turpin. Nevison, alias Nicks, usually operated near Gad's Hill, Gravesend, catching sailors recently paid off at Chatham, but in a tale related by Daniel Defoe[2] he fled a robbery in 1676 fearing he had been identified and seeking an alibi elsewhere. It is said he left Gravesend at 4am and rode through Chelmsford, Braintree, Cambridge, Huntingdon and on to York, which he reached during the afternoon. With an alibi established, he was nevertheless later charged with the robbery and duly acquitted, after which he acquired the nickname 'Swift' Nicks. The ride to York, however, is often attributed to Turpin (1706-1739), the son of an Essex innkeeper who went into partnership on the Cambridge road with highwayman Tom King, and whom he later shot and killed, allegedly by accident. Turpin fled the scene and in July, 1737[73] arrived at Long Sutton in south Lincolnshire, calling himself John Palmer and describing himself as a horse dealer

and butcher. 'Palmer' is said to have operated in the area for about nine months before a local magistrate, his suspicions roused by a bout of local sheep stealing, began to ask questions. Turpin moved on again, this time to York, where he was finally arrested and hanged.

Those who were caught and convicted inevitably faced the gallows, many of which outside the capital were erected at prominent cross-roads on the outskirts of towns. In Norfolk,[74] gallows are known to have stood at Gallows Hill, just outside Thetford, and probably at Gallows Hill, Hargham, and Galley Hill, close to the Peddars Way near East Wretham. Doubtless there were many more. John Keane[75] says the Thetford gallows, at a place on Gallows Hill known as the Wilderness, not far from Tom Paine's cottage, were certainly in use in 1737, the year Paine was born. Many of the hangings were held in the spring, following Lent Assizes. Sometimes the bodies of executed criminals were hung beside the road, usually in chains or in a metal cage, as an example to passers-by. Again, the gibbets were often located at cross-roads, places which rapidly became associated with folklore and superstition. And some were buried in similar spots, again providing ammunition for local tales of mystery and horror. Certainly where madness could not be proved, the bodies of suicides were often buried at cross-roads, sometimes at night. Anyone who committed suicide while in control of his or her mental facilities was considered felo-de-se (a felon of oneself), deserving of punishment as a murderer. For example, it is said that in 1823[2] a certain John Mortland, a murderer, committed suicide and was buried at cross-roads in St John's Wood, London, opposite what is now Lord's cricket ground.

Norfolk has a number of such sombre sites. Robert Halliday[110] lists Nobb's Corner (at the boundary of Hempnall, Topcroft and Woodton), the grave of Richard Nobbs who hanged himself in 1785 while suspected of murder; St Benedict's crossroads, Norwich (the graves of drowned Susanna Gooch, 1786, and the hanged John Stimpson, 1794); and Harleston (at Lush's Bush, between Redenhall and Harleston), the grave of Mary Turrel who swallowed arsenic in 1813 after the body of a baby was found. Other similar burials included those of Bradley Saunders of Lynn, who took laudanum, and Stephen Cutting of Banham, who drowned. Local graves of uncertain origin include Crosses Grave (Harpley, Rudham), Bugg's Grave (Horsford, Drayton), Pigg's Grave (Melton Constable, Briningham, a possible gallows site), and Chunk Harvey's Grave (Thetford, Euston), said to be the grave of a pirate but more likely that of a Thetford carpenter named Thomas Harvey. The practice of roadside burial was abolished in 1823. By about 1840 the 'Bloody Code,' with its innumerable list of capital offences, including stocks, gibbets and pillories, had also been abolished, and from 1868 executions were carried out in private. Even so, when Faden's map[34] was published in 1797 he could still list a set of gallows at Gallows Hill, Thetford, and several gibbets, including one between Martham and Hemsby, one near West Dereham on the road to Crimplesham, and another between Yarmouth and Caister.

DROVERS

Droving seems to have seen its biggest period of expansion in the 16th century when many expanding towns and cities began to establish markets where cattle were sold on for fattening before re-sale to urban slaughterhouses. Indeed, the work expanded so greatly that from 1552 drovers had to be licensed, gaining in the process a reputation for integrity. Cattle droves became a recognised way of transferring money, so the drovers dealt in promissory notes and bills. A Welsh drovers' bank eventually became a subsidiary of Lloyd's Bank, whose black horse emblem still commemorates the link. Generally, the drovers worked in teams, a herd of about 200 cattle sometimes being divided into units of 50, each with one man in charge. For long journeys the cattle were shod, while geese, an East Anglian speciality for the London Christmas market, had to endure a coating of sawdust, sand and tar on their feet. Avoiding the harder surfaces of the turnpikes and declining to pay the tolls, the drovers, accompanied by their dogs and ponies, tended to use the unmade lanes and tracks, covering perhaps 12 miles a day. The need for water, overnight grazing, lodging and refreshment also saw the establishment of networks of drovers' inns, some in remote areas. At its peak it was a huge industry with thousands of cattle being moved from farms and pastures to markets. In the 1840s Scottish cattle, mainly Galloway bullocks, were driven to East Norfolk and re-fattened over winter on the marshes before being assembled again near the Brick Kiln Inn, Little Plumstead, ready for the April drive to London's Smithfield market. Norfolk's largest clearing house, and the main target for the Scottish herds, was the annual fair at Horsham St Faith, a huge, centuries-old affair. Held on the feast day of St Faith, latterly October 6, and known as Fay's Fair,[76] it attracted enormous crowds and big herds. There were other Scottish cattle fairs at Setchey - where the herds entered Norfolk - Halesworth, Hempton Green (near Fakenham) and Hoxne. The trade began to die in the mid- and late-19th century, when the railways came, and many of the old drovers' inns were forced to close. St Faith's fair itself ended in 1830, by which time it had been replaced by Norwich cattle market. Even this market, which may date to the 13th century and which was re-affirmed by a charter of 1462,[77] is now perceived as being under economic threat despite a move some years ago from its traditional site beside Norwich castle to Hall Road. Other cattle markets at Acle, North Walsham, Reepham and King's Lynn have closed in recent years.

The drovers, used to roughing it in all weathers, were colourful characters, earning themselves reputations for trustworthiness and hard drinking. Scottish drovers, relieved of their responsibilities at St Faith's, or Norwich, are said to have ordered their dogs to head north ahead of their own return. And one Norwich drover, at the end of a seven-day 'drift' to London, evidently decided to stay over in the capital. He sent his dog home with a note on its collar asking landlords at his regular pubs to feed and water it, saying he would pay them next time he called. The system worked well, apparently. Locally, the legacy of the drovers is sparse for no specifically created drovers' roads are known. They tended to use the green and unmade lanes. An occasional pub name, roads marked as 'droves' or 'drifts,' and some place-names such as Bullock Hill, are all that mark their passing. Harling Drove Road, which runs from the Fen borders to cross the Peddars Way on Roudham Heath, and a road of largely unknown origin, was certainly used by some drovers who took advantage of available watering facilities at the nearby Breck meres.

CARRIERS
Carriers were a traditional lifeline for many small communities, for their carts, vans, fly's and waggons provided passenger and delivery services essential for the survival of rural populations. Nearly every village had at least one, or a carrier who passed through regularly. Many of them used vehicles similar to farm waggons, except that they were less robust, had narrower wheels, and were fitted with a canvas awning, or tilt, supported by wooden hoops. In Norwich, they were once a familiar sight parked and waiting for passengers and loads in Ber Street or St Benedict's.[78] Rumbling along at three or four miles an hour they carried people, goods, and even articles 'on approval,' and nearly every town and village advertised regular services. In Attleborough, for example, they regularly used the Griffin Inn, whose carriage entrance still exists. Once, it would also have had stables, hay lofts and rooms for travellers. So familiar and known were they, in fact, that when one well-known Norwich-London carrier, John Webster, died, his passing was mentioned in the Attleborough parish registers.[79] He was a regular user of the Griffin. Ultimately, the carrier service proved more adaptable than that offered by packmen and drovers, for most of them survived the railway age. Instead of giving up, the carts promptly ran services to and from the new railway stations, once again establishing valuable rural links. Indeed, White's Directory of 1845[80] is stuffed with details of them. Martham for example, is shown as having had two services to Norwich and one to Yarmouth; Shipdham had carrier services to Norwich three times a week and London four times a week; while New Buckenham, in addition to a weekly coach to Norwich, also had carrier waggons

The Griffin Hotel at Attleborough, with its carriers' entrance (right).

to Norwich (four weekly), Bury St Edmunds (two) and Kenninghall (two). In general, carriers survived until the 1920s when they were finally driven out of business by motorised coaches and lorries.

PITS, PONDS and MERES

Pit, or pit-hole, is a Norfolk word for a pond, and they have a long history as sources of water in many farms and villages (Great Massingham, for example). Rackham[50] suggests that one of the largest concentrations of ponds in agricultural landscapes occurs on the boulder clays of south and mid-Norfolk and north-east Suffolk. Many have been drained and obliterated by farming operations, while some villages now see them as amenity and wildlife areas. The mere, from an Old English place-name element meaning lake or pool, also has a particular place in the fabric of Norfolk. Diss, for example, grew up alongside its mere, while Seamere, near Hingham, is isolated in comparison. Some of the Breckland meres clearly had important roles as suppliers of water in what was otherwise an essentially dry heathland area. For example, six parish boundaries meet at Ringmere, which was also mentioned in the Heimskringla Saga as the site of a battle in AD1010, and Ringmere and Langmere seem to have been used to water stock being escorted on the nearby Harling Drove Road. Indeed, one interpretation of the Norfolk dialect word 'mardle,' which has come to mean 'gossip,' is 'animal watering-hole.' Other meres in the vicinity include Langmere, Fenmere, and the Devil's Punchbowl. Pingoes, some of which can be seen on Thompson Common and other places, are thought to be depressions formed by the melt material from underground lenses of ice. Marl-pits are sometimes mistaken for ponds. Most often seen as tree-fringed pits, or as depressions in arable fields, they relate to the practice of digging marl to spread on the fields, often with manure, which went on from medieval times through to the end of the 19th century. A great many marl-pits can be seen from the Peddars Way in west and north-west Norfolk.

GREEN LANES
In basic terms green lanes are unmade roads, sometimes lined by trees or hedgerows - the 'white roads' of the Ordnance Survey maps - and they invariably present two problems. One is actually defining what is a green lane. The other is in attempting to date them. The first is covered, albeit tentatively, in the opening sentence of this section, but I have to confess ignorance over the second. Some are doubtless of very great antiquity, having endured perhaps as long as Roman streets, while others may have come into being during the 17th century. Another way of looking at it is to say that today's green lanes are leftovers from the 1920s/30s when parish councils were asked to supply the county council with lists of lanes they wanted tarring. In other words, 1998's survivals simply survived because they were not listed for the tarring programme. Even today it is still possible to see one result of these programmes, namely, lanes with widely set verges and hedges where the hard surface snakes thinly in between, the old cattle width having been wider than the area for which money was available for tarring. Addison[28] points out that the Countryside Act of 1968 re-classified green lanes as footpaths, bridle ways and byways. The effect was to strip them of the protection usually accorded lanes or highways. In consequence many have disappeared, largely through ploughing, while others survive as field entrances or boundaries. Norfolk's 1976 return to the Department of Transport[81] showed the county then had over 250 miles of unsurfaced roads and green lanes, and while the total length may have reduced further in the last 20 years or so a few do still survive, though not necessarily intact.

They are worth searching for, and they are surely worth protecting, for green lanes offer us a glimpse of what most roads used to look like, and indeed, what most non-major roads did look like prior to the 20th century. The irony is that despite their having been the backbone of our rural communications systems for centuries they are now hugely neglected, sparsely researched and largely forgotten. Those that have escaped the tyranny of the bulldozer and the plough seem to have

no role other than to delight
the walker and offer respite
to wildlife. Thus they are
increasingly   vulnerable.
Alas, we have allowed the
green lanes - which once
offered generations of foot-
sore peasants the means of
moving from one village to
another - to slip into
obscurity, and by and large
we   have   forgotten   their
lore, once such a vibrant
part of our rural heritage.

MILLS and PUMPS
It   seems   likely   that
windmills were numerous
by the end of the 12th
century, one theory being
that they were introduced
from Europe by travellers
returning from the Holy
Land. Essentially, there are
only   three   or   four
categories of corn mill.
First   came   the   fixed

A drainage mill beside the Thurne.

structure, which operated only when the wind was in a particular direction. The
post mill was a big improvement, for the sails revolved on a central post so they
could be orientated to catch the wind. A wheel and tail pole at the rear held the
sails into the wind after they had been pushed into position by hand. Post mills
also enclosed raised mounds, to support the central machinery, and on sites, often
on exposed hillsides, where the mill structure has disappeared the mounds are
sometimes interpreted as tumuli. Towards the end of the medieval period the
round house, which protected the grinding machinery, was sometimes given a
brick base or even extended upwards, to become known as the smock or tower mill.
By the 19th century the tower mill, with its tarred brick tower, was the most
common design. Faden's map of 1797[(34)] depicts nearly 260 windmills in Norfolk,
though by 1912 there were only about 100 left. Just before the outbreak of the

Second World War the number had dwindled to eleven, the main threats having been agricultural depression and the advent of steam and diesel-driven machinery. Some mills (Wicklewood, Denver, Billingford, Little Cressingham, Old Buckenham, for example) are in the care of the Norfolk Windmills Trust; others (eg Ringstead, Cley, Weybourne) have been converted to residential use; while about 50 others are derelict, stumps, or down to foundation level.

Not all mills handled corn, for the structures were also used for bone-crushing, sawing, cement grinding, starch milling, crushing cole seed, snuff milling, spinning yarn, and so on. Fragments of grinding stones, sometimes with a pattern of grooves incised on the top (to assist an even spread of corn), most of them dating from the 18th and 19th centuries, can be spotted in gardens or being used as gateposts. Occasionally, lumps of an imported aggregate known as puddingstone also turn up. Often ploughed out and then discarded at the edges of fields, these were used to grind corn during the Roman period.

Watermills, possibly introduced by the Romans, were numerous in the Saxon period and some 6000 were recorded nationally by the Domesday Survey. There are essentially four types: horizontal, where water was directed by chute to the paddles; undershot, a Roman innovation, where the wheel had flat blades and was in contact with the water at the bottom; overshot, developed during the Middle Ages, where water was introduced at the top; and breastshot, where water was directed into 'buckets' at axle height. Over 100 watermill sites are known in Norfolk,[10] though fewer than 20 retain their waterwheels and machinery. Another 35 or so have been converted to other uses. Some, such as Lakenham, Cringleford, Mundesley, Horstead,

A green lane near Blickling.

Hardingham and Buxton, have at various times been destroyed or damaged by fire.

Drainage mills, or wind pumps, were introduced into the Fens and the Broads probably towards the end of the 17th century as a means of lifting water from one level to the next. In their heyday in the 19th century there were said to be over 120 in Broadland alone, one of the greatest concentrations in the country. By 1920 about 30 were still working on Halvergate marsh, but the last, as they were steadily

A drainage channel near Catfield.

superseded by steam, diesel and electricity, ceased in 1953. Over 60 of the surviving examples[36] are brick tower mills, while the others are timber, but all of them may have been rebuilt and re-fitted many times. Two of the oldest (Oby and Brograve Level) are now fitted with turbine pumps. Berney Arms, built in 1865, is the biggest.

WORKHOUSES

The 'pauper palaces' were buried deep in the subconcious of former generations, fearful they might one day end up in such places, particularly if they became too old to work or to support themselves. The bleakness of life in the workhouses, and the association with vagrancy, struck terror in many elderly hearts. In 1576 an Act ordered towns to acquire a store of materials - hitherto, the poor were given 'out-relief,' including money, clothing, food and fuel - while another of 1597 encouraged the provision of 'abiding and working houses.' King's Lynn for example, converted a medieval chapel. Thus the parishes, now responsible for the relief of poverty, gradually acquired poor houses. Workhouses became more common after 1722, when it was made easier to provide them, but by 1776 Norfolk still had only 24. The cost of relief was rising, and by 1803 Norfolk was spending £45,000 a year on some 4000 residents in 130 workhouses. Seeking economies, some parishes and some Hundreds teamed up to provide central Houses of Industry. The Poor Law Amendment Act of 1834 provided new Unions and sought to provide equal-sized geographical areas of responsibility, but the theory was easier than the practice. In the 1830s a dozen Unions built new workhouses, including Lingwood, Pulham St Mary, Docking and Kenninghall, to a variety of designs. They were finally designated as Poor Law institutions in 1913, while in 1929 local authorities were encouraged to convert them to hospitals. The Poor Law 'palaces' after 1834 included: King's Lynn, Downham Market, Docking, Gayton, Swaffham, Thetford, Great Snoring, Gressenhall, Rockland, Kenninghall, West Beckham, Aylsham, Smallburgh, Horsham St Faith, Rollesby, Lingwood, Yarmouth, Wicklewood, Pulham St Mary, Swainsthorpe, Norwich and Heckingham. Following an Act of 1948 which established old peoples' homes, many of the 'palaces' went into private hands, were converted into museums, or were simply abandoned.

CANALS, STAUNCHES and WHERRIES

Tributaries of the Waveney, Bure, Yare and Great Ouse were used for navigation until the Late Saxon period, when many of them were evidently blocked by the construction of watermills. However, artificial cuts dug in the late Middle Ages increased water access in the Fens, and from the 17th century Acts of Parliament helped raise capital for river improvements such as the installation of locks (enabling boats to bypass the watermills), embanking the rivers, digging cut-offs, and dredging. Many local rivers, including the Nar, Little Ouse, the Waveney from Beccles to Bungay, and the upper Bure to Aylsham, benefited.[10] The great age of canal building began early in the 18th century and 'peaked' in the 1790s, during which time, nationally at least, 42[37] new canals were dug. Norfolk was comparatively slow to respond. Back in 1656 Francis Matthew[36] had argued for the creation of a link between Yarmouth and King's Lynn, by improving the course of the Waveney and Little Ouse and the digging of a canal near Lopham and Redgrave, but nothing came of the idea. Ultimately, the most important new local waterways were the North Walsham and Dilham canal, from Dilham to Antingham, which opened in 1826, and the Norwich and Lowestoft Navigation, whose 1833 New Cut from Reedham to Haddiscoe joined sections of the Yare and Waveney to a new harbour at Lowestoft. This enabled sea-going vessels to reach Norwich without paying Yarmouth tolls or having to brave the Breydon mud flats. River navigation by shallow draft keelboat, and rowing boat and punt, allowed up to 30 tons to be moved inland, but the 19th century introduction of the trading wherry - the last of which, the Ella, was launched in 1912 - increased tonnages to 60 tons on the Yare and Waveney. Grain, peat, marl, hay, dung, lime and consumer goods were all traded, particularly from Yarmouth and Lynn, to inland centres. On the canals, 'passage' or 'packet' boats carried goods and passengers.

A sluice, incidentally, is a channel carrying a rapid current of water, often with a sluice gate to control the flow. A staunch was quite different. In 1925 there were only 32 staunches in England, some 26 of them in the Fens, eight of which were on the Little Ouse, including sites at Thetford, Croxton, Santon and Brandon. In effect, they served the same purpose as locks. According to R Rainbird Clarke[82] staunches had oak doors which were raised by chains on an axle. At one end was a large wheel. The operator simply trod the spokes to revolve the axle, wind the chains, and thus raise or lower the doors.

RAILWAY MANIA

As with canals and turnpikes, Norfolk responded rather slowly to the latest mania, and it was not until 1844 that the Yarmouth and Norwich Railway opened its new line. A year later a Norwich-Brandon link was completed, establishing a direct link with London. Thereafter several rail systems, centred on Lynn and Ipswich, also spread from Norwich to serve Fakenham and Lowestoft; and by 1850 most of Norfolk's main centres, aside from the North Norfolk coast, had been linked. The effect on the landscape and the rural population, with heavy machinery and gangs of navvies building bridges, cuttings, embankments and laying the lines, must have been enormous. Certainly it was a civil engineering programme of a scale not seen again until the building of dozens of airfields at the onset of the Second World War. There were a number of mergings and creations, including the Great Eastern Railway, but by the 1870s it was evident that the fragile state of the old Eastern Counties Railway was holding back investment. Then its regional monopoly was broken by independent lines built from Lynn to Fakenham and Yarmouth to North Walsham, from whence they eventually joined at Melton Constable, in 1883, and then extended to Norwich and Cromer. This grid formed the Midland & Great Northern Joint Railway, whose competition finally sparked the GER to improve many of its lines, including a faster link for East Dereham to London via Wymondham and Forncett. Such was the intensity and the popularity of the railway programme that by 1906 Blakeney was the only Norfolk place of size more than five miles from a station.

Despite initial discomforts for passengers, especially those in the 3rd class open trucks, rail travel quickly became the main means of travel for the mass of the population. Haulage also became faster and cheaper, mail deliveries were more efficient, small villages suddenly had direct links with London, mass tourism began, and livestock farmers benefited even if local fat stock markets suffered in consequence. The reverse of the coin was that the stage coaches, stripped of business, were swept from the roads and the coaching inns replaced by railway hotels. It is difficult to assess the pros and cons, but places like East Dereham, Yarmouth, Cromer, North Walsham, Wymondham and Fakenham seemed to benefit from the coming of the railways while Swaffham (now merely a station on a through route), Cley, Loddon and Hingham probably did not. Meanwhile, on the roads, there was little to be seen other than waggons and the occasional carriers' cart. Inevitably, the monopoly and popularity of the railways was in turn broken, for in the 1920s bus and motor transport services began to expand. Passenger services on the Upwell and Stoke Ferry rail lines stopped in 1927/31, and other services were abandoned in the 1950s. There were further savage cuts in 1964/68, after which some lines were torn up and many railway properties adapted to other uses.

TOURISM and FISHING

Yarmouth's herring fishing industry has invariably been of national importance, even though Lynn and Yarmouth vessels dabbled in Icelandic cod fishery during the 17th century. Both centres also went into Arctic whaling in the mid-17th and late 18th centuries, and the operation continued at Lynn until late into the 19th century. Closer home, cockles, mussels, oysters, whelks, shrimps, crabs and lobsters have been fished commercially from small ports and creeks around the Norfolk coast, though only three or four small inshore fleets actually survive today. Yarmouth and Lynn, with their inland agricultural connections, have always been Norfolk's main trading ports, while Blakeney, Cley and Wells once served North Norfolk and smaller vessels traded from beaches and creeks. Herring, however, was an important Yarmouth export until well into the 20th century. Early on, and during a season which lasted 10 weeks from September, upwards of 200 Yarmouth vessels were involved, while the gutting and curing in innumerable curing houses attracted workers from away. Yarmouth's annual invasion by Scots' lassies was one of the 'highlights' of the year. In more recent decades Yarmouth maritime interests have been more closely aligned with natural gas exploration and the maintenance of gas installations, the main terminal being at Bacton.

In the 18th century country gentry and fashionable society began to seek out the Norfolk coast for leisure and sea-water bathing. Yarmouth, one of the first places to grow, built a Bath House in 1759 and also began to erect buildings along the shoreline, a move which was not immediately universally popular. Then Cromer, a small fishing village, also began to attract a select clientele, and it built a Bath House in 1814. Once the bathing machines began to appear, then other watering places also began to cater for visitors, developing places to stay, entertainment, and even distinctive seaside architecture. As for the beginnings of the local tourism

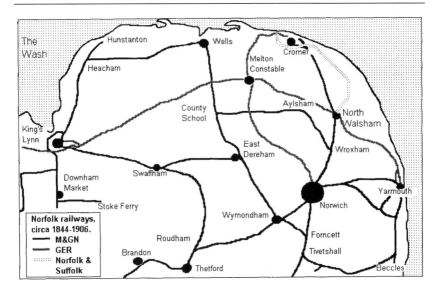

industry, it can be argued[55] this can be traced to June 30, 1846, when schoolchildren from Attleborough, Wymondham and Norwich were conveyed to Yarmouth for the day by the new-fangled railway for 3d. In truth there were a number of factors involved in a growing demand for leisure and travel, including an expanding middle class, the creation of Bank Holidays in 1870, and a growing desire to escape urban drudgery, albeit briefly. But the railway was the key, and frankly, no resort could hope to be successful without a train station. For example, New Hunstanton, a creation on a green field site, only really became popular when the rail link through Lynn and Sandringham arrived. Then in the 1880s London journalist Clement Scott, writing of the Cromer and Overstrand area, inadvertently invented the romantic Poppyland image, and the real boom began. Hotels were built and the trippers flocked in, Overstrand expanding as a fashionable nearby suburb. Norfolk's most important Victorian resorts were New Hunstanton, Sheringham, Cromer and Yarmouth, though Wells, Overstrand and Mundesley had their supporters. The fishing communities were never the same again.

STONEBREAKERS
Like the road sweeper, the stonebreaker has earned his niche in any history of our highways. Sometimes working in gangs, sometimes a lonely figure crouched on the verge, the stonebreaker with his pick and hammer helped keep the roads in

trim for many decades, or at least during the period from the latter end of the turnpike era through to the arrival of the bicycle and the mechanical tarring of country lanes. Road repairs were often carried out at the whim of local parish or local landowner, and the collection of stones and the filling of potholes, allied to a steady supply of cheap labour, made it one of the most advantageous methods. Recalling 1771, and writing almost one hundred years later, JE Austin Leigh[2] said: 'In those days it was not unusual to set men to work with shovel and pickaxe to fill up ruts and holes in roads seldom used by carriages, and on such special occasions as a funeral or wedding.' In 1901 William Dutt[101] recorded that near Wickham Market (Suffolk) he encountered an old road-mender breaking flints by the roadside. 'He will be 80 years old 'come next October', he tells me, and can remember the time when the two-horse waggons which, before the era of railways, conveyed fish from Yarmouth and Lowestoft to 'Lunnun,' used to run too and fro along this road.' This venerable stonebreaker, who wore a tattered military overcoat, told Dutt his father 'come from out Dareham way and was in the West Norfolk Militia in his time.' And Ben Ripper[46] said his father could remember the dusty, unmetalled way from Swaffham to Cockley Cley, and gangs of women and boys being employed in the fields as stone pickers. This was also in about 1900. They gathered the stones in bottomless baskets which, when lifted, left heaps of stones ready to be gathered and used on the road.

But it is a roadside glimpse of a solitary stonebreaker, poorly paid and an object of pity, who catches the imagination. Michael Fairless[8] endeavoured to anoint him and his backbreaking toil with a veneer of nobility by making him content with his lot, blessed even, immersed in 'the companionship of solitude.' In some areas of the country small mossy roadside mounds of stones and occasional little hollows, from which the stones were extracted, are all that remain to remind us of the unremitting toil of the stonebreaker and his callused hands. In the early 1900s experiments with tar and gravel began, again leaving the stonebreakers on the sidelines. For some years, however, county councils maintained major roads by a system of roadmen who worked for a number of miles on each side of their home.

GENTLEMEN of the ROAD
Pedlars (or travelling salesmen) and tramps (along with hitch-hikers and vagrants) have been on the road for centuries, and even during the Second World War they were still to be seen. As a child in south Lincolnshire in the 1940s I can recall a scissors grinder passing by during the summer months, calling for custom by ringing a bell; a gypsy peg lady knocking on the back door and failing to persuade my mother to buy either charms or pegs on the grounds that if she bought anything every passing peg-seller would call; and the occasional tramp, walking from one

night shelter to another, who sometimes slept in the hedgerows and who called to beg for a pinch of tea or a tot of milk. I recall being terrified of them, for some reason, but they were invariably polite, charming chaps who always doffed their caps and who were usually rewarded with a warm cuppa and some milk to take away.

The first gypsies seem to have reached England at the beginning of the 16th century, when they were known as Gypcians or Gipsons, because it was thought these dark-skinned people with their horses, dogs, tents and vans, their knowledge of metal-working and their colourful, travelling life, had come from Egypt. Later it was demonstrated that their language, Romany, shared common features with Sanskrit and later Indian languages, to which had been added other words and meanings as they migrated across Europe from the south-east during the late medieval period. So they may originally have been a nomadic Indian people who lived by seasonal work, itinerant trade, and by providing entertainment, such as fortune telling. They have endured numerous periods of persecution, for being Catholics, for being different, or simply for being gypsies. One 1993 estimate[111] suggested there were then 80,000 of them in England. As for the Romany language, a gaujo is a non-Romany person; grai, a horse; vardo, a caravan; patrins, means a roadside sign or indicator to other gypsies; yog, is a stick fire; and kushti means good. Some slightly more recognisable words include tatting (rag collecting), mush (man), stir (prison), chop and change (swap, exchange), and lorry (four-wheeled waggon pulled by a horse). Incidentally, a tinker is a Scots and Irish word most accurately used to describe an itinerant repairer of kettles and pans. The extraordinary George Borrow, born in Norfolk in 1803 and who died a recluse at Oulton Broad, lived with the gypsies for a time and wrote a number of books about them, including Lavengro and Romany Rye. Despite several attempts I have found both titles too dry for my taste, but I can claim to have met three or four Romany people, including the much-travelled Gordon Boswell,[83] who died at Spalding in 1977; Eli Frankham, a campaigner for Romany rights, then living near Walpole St Andrew; and a 'settled' Romany living near Hevingham, who showed me round his caravan still parked in his bungalow garden, full of extraordinary glassware.

In recent decades the Romany influence has become seriously diluted, first, by gypsies wanting to settle (for some, 'the height of ambition is wanting a letter box,' as Eli Frankham once told me) because modern pressures (eg, motor traffic, planning regulations, bureaucracy, shortage of camp sites and seasonal work, public hostility) had made life on the road uneconomic and intolerable, and second, because of an influx of other and not always welcome categories of travellers including Irish tinkers, diddicoys (not true Romanies), New Age freaks, the unemployed, the unemployable and the homeless. Thus it is not always easy, on seeing a camp, to tell whether or not they are a genuine group of gypsies. Tip: Romany camps are usually tidy, their caravans pristine and gleaming. Many have now settled in the Fens, where they find part-time work, or around the edges of Mousehold, a favourite haunt in generations past. The gypsy has been a significant element in the country landscape for centuries, and their general passing from the rural scene means another splash of colour has dulled.

WOODLAND and HEDGEROWS
Wayland Wood, near Watton, the largest block of ancient woodland in Norfolk, is said to go back to Domesday. In fact it was the Wayland Hundred which was recorded, not the wood. However, the name Wayland seems to be derived from the Viking word wanelund, which meant wood, or even sacred grove. So the wood's antiquity is not in doubt. It is still managed[84] in the traditional way as coppice with oak standards, and remains a rare example of the wildwood which once covered much of lowland Britain. Honeypot Wood, near Wendling, also has a long tradition of traditional management, with oak/ash standards and hazel/field maple coppice. Honeypot Wood also houses some surviving concrete bunkers and rides built for bomb storage for the Second World War air base at nearby Wendling. Tyrrel's Wood, near Pulham Market, is another ancient block of woodland, while Thursford Wood is primarily of mature oak, some pollarded. Thetford's forests were initially planted between the wars when a heightened demand for timber coincided with low land prices, enabling the Forestry Commission to buy many hundreds of acres. These forests are flourishing, in contrast to many of Breckland's Scots pines, which are now very old, and many of Norfolk's oaks, which are largely past maturity and have either died or developed a stag-headed configuration. In recent decades, too, the county's elms have been badly hit by Dutch Elm disease.

Some 25 years ago research by the University of East Anglia showed that between 1946 and 1970 more than 8450 miles[85] of Norfolk hedgerow had been removed. Fortunately, the pace of destruction has slackened, but huge areas of rural Norfolk now bear witness to the rush to develop larger field units and barrier-free verges capable of withstanding the manoeuvrings of ever heavier pieces of agricultural machinery. Some hedgerows undoubtedly date to the medieval period; a few may be even older. In the Tivetshall and Scole areas, for example, some field boundaries and lane patterns are thought to relate to the Roman period or even the Iron Ages. But assessing the age of hedges is a thorny business, for although the Hooper species-counting method is widely used it is evidently not a completely accurate indicator in every case. Silvia Addington,[86] researching hedgerows in Tasburgh, concluded that in this area it was the combination of species, and not the number, that was the better indicator. For example, she found that hedges with a high ratio of thorns were generally not as old as those mainly of elm, hazel, maple, ash, and 20 per cent thorn. Ancient hedges seem to have originated from a number of sources. Along with walls, ditches, fences, and earth banks, they have been used to control stock and mark properties and routes perhaps since the Neolithic. Some are the 'ghosts' of woodland clearance, where a margin of trees was left to mark field boundaries. Others were planted as a result of land enclosures or as part of the development from common to open field. Still more may have arrived by accident, for Rackham[50] has noted they arise wherever people are few and acres are many, especially in times of moderate agricultural depression. When a ditch, a bank or a boundary not far from a source of wood seed is neglected for a few years then a hedge will probably result. Fences can also turn into hedges through birds perching and dropping seeds. In fact, Rackham concludes, perhaps one quarter of English hedges may have arisen naturally, chiefly at times of agricultural recession and neglect.

DEFENCES, PILLBOXES and TANK TRAPS

In 1539, fearful of invasions from France or the Low Countries, Henry V111 turned local responsibility into a national strategy when he ordered a defence review of the country's coastline. In Norfolk, King's Lynn, Weybourne and Yarmouth were deemed in need of protection, the last two because of deep water anchorages close to shore. All that happened, however, was that two gun batteries were built at Yarmouth. Fifty years later, when the Armada threatened, precisely the same places were considered vulnerable, though by this time Lynn had a small fort, there was an earth fort at Weybourne, and Yarmouth's defences had been strengthened. Plans to further extend the defences at Lynn and Weybourne were put on hold when the Armada was defeated. In 1642, at the time of the Civil War, Norfolk declared for Parliament though Lynn later changed its mind and switched sides. At the time, Norwich had its town walls, so as a precaution some of the gates were blocked and guns placed on the castle mound. Lynn possessed a strong fortress, with earthwork extensions to its medieval walls, while Yarmouth also had its walls. In addition, the Armada defences were repaired and new earthworks and batteries built to defend the Roads. In 1778, when France, Spain and Holland joined in the row over our American colonies, batteries were installed at Cromer and Yarmouth, and the Lynn fort was re-armed, but the Napoleonic War of 1803 was seen as a much greater threat. This time there were defensive works at Cromer, Mundesley and Holkham,[10] and beach exits were blocked. All of them were disarmed by the 1850s, leaving Norfolk with no effective coastal defences at all.

During the early stages of the First World War troops were quickly deployed at Weybourne. Then in November, 1914, Yarmouth was bombarded by the German Fleet and the area became a hive of activity. Defences were dug across Sheringham golf course, with reserve lines of defence between Briston and Hunworth, while guns were installed at Weybourne, Cromer and Mundesley and, in 1916, at Gorleston. Circular concrete pillboxes were also built from Weybourne to Sea Palling, while others, resembling the more familiar Second World War design, were installed landward of Yarmouth. In 1940, though Norfolk was thought to be vulnerable to diversionary attacks by the enemy, the British army was forced to adopt a largely static role. By 1942 some 14 coastal batteries comprising 28 guns had been installed in areas such as Terrington, Hunstanton, Brancaster, Wells, Cley, Weybourne, Cromer, Mundesley, Happisburgh and Yarmouth - some of them camouflaged as haystacks, or inside 'houses' with false roofs - while the beaches were protected by miles of scaffolding at the water's edge, concrete blocks and anti-tank mines. There were also lines of trenches and pillboxes among the dunes and on cliff-tops. Inland, there were five lines of pillbox defence, the first three based on the rivers Ant, Bure and Wensum, the fourth on the Yare and the fifth on the Ouse. Norwich, meanwhile, was surrounded by anti-tank obstacles and half a dozen pillboxes.

My war-time childhood was spent in south Lincolnshire, not Norwich, but I can recall pillbox road blocks and tank traps - usually large cubes of concrete -

An overgrown wartime pillbox at Halvergate.

positioned ready on the verges, and one of the 'false roof' houses. Towards the end of the war, after the guns had gone, we used to play in it. It was made of timber, painted to look like a bungalow, and had a section in the timber roof which could be slid open. Deserted pillboxes still litter the Norfolk countryside, and it is still possible to find concrete tank traps dragged into the undergrowth beside roads, some of the most recent I have seen being on the Brampton side of the Bure bridge at Oxnead. There is a pillbox close by.

MILITARY MATTERS

Yarmouth was a minor Naval base during both world wars, but the Army was very prominent, most particularly in the coastal defence zones and in Breckland, where a great deal of training took place. There had been military activity on the Breck heaths since early this century. In 1911, for example, during the East Anglian manoeuvres, some 30,000 infantrymen camped on Thetford Warren, and during the war tanks were tested in the vicinity. In 1940 the War Department acquired land near Thetford for troop training, but it proved insufficient for live firing exercises. So in 1942 the Stanford Battle Area was established. It meant the closure of the Thetford-Watton main road, the extinction of the villages of West Tofts, Buckenham Tofts, Tottington, Stanford, Langford and Sturston, and the evacuation of some 600 inhabitants. The land was compulsorily acquired by the military in 1950, and the area was extended again in 1990. Today, the Battle Area has an annual through-put[87] of some 85,000 troops, 5 million rounds of ammunition, 15,000 vehicle and 1000 helicopter movements.

Norfolk's place in aviation history is even more substantial than this, however. Aircraft used Snare Hill prior to the First World War; between the wars there were aerodromes at Feltwell, Watton, Mildenhall, and other places; but it reached its zenith during the Second World War when the RAF, Allied Air Forces and the United States' 8th Air Force were based in East Anglia in strength. The subject is too big to go into here, and not altogether relevant. Suffice to say that the runway building programme was a huge civil engineering undertaking, that the Norfolk countryside is still littered with active bases and the remains of many more closed after the war, and that according to Derek Johnson[88] Norfolk's Second World War air bases included: Attlebridge, Bircham Newton, Bodney, Coltishall, Deopham, Docking, Downham Market, East Wretham, Feltwell, Fersfield, Great Massingham, Hardwick, Hethel, Horsham St Faith, Longham, Little Snoring, Ludham, Marham, Matlaske, Methwold, North Creake, North Pickenham, Old Buckenham, Oulton, Pulham, Rackheath, Sculthorpe, Seething, Shipdham, Snetterton, Swanton Morley, Swannington, Thorpe Abbots, Tibenham, Watton, Wendling, West Raynham and Weybourne.

SMALLHOLDINGS

An odd subject, perhaps, and yet the origins of this particular land movement go back to the 1860s, while the 'land question' was actually the political hot potato of the 1880s. More-over, Norfolk County Council, once it became involved,[42] ultimately became a significant force in the area of land ownership. Calls for a radical re-distribution of land, from big landowners to small farmers, found one supporter in Sir Richard Winfrey, elected Liberal MP for South West Norfolk in 1906. By this time he had already formed a smallholders' association, and he acquired land at Swaffham and Downham Market for farm workers. An Act giving smallholdings' responsibility to local councils was passed just as the agricultural depression was at its worst, but after a slow start Norfolk finally bought land at Nordelph. By the end of 1909 some 2550 acres had been acquired and nearly 270 tenants were renting. Further acres were either bought or leased at, among other places, Outwell, Stalham, Great Massingham, Binham, Wiggenhall, St Mary Magdalen and Stow Bardolph, until by the outbreak of the First World War over 9640 acres were on the county's books. Another player in the drama was Sir George Edwards, in 1909 secretary of the Norfolk Agricultural Labourers' Union, and later MP, who obtained over a thousand acres near Walsingham and put 115 men to work. Yet another advocate for reform was RM Bacon, then editor of the Norwich Mercury,[89] who wanted to use public money to establish labourers with property of their own. It was a hotly debated political issue for many years. During the inter-war years Norfolk seems to have been somewhat more enthusiastic over the matter, until by 1923 some 23,000 acres[42] were under its control - overseen by its own smallholdings' department - which made it the biggest landowner in Norfolk next to the Holkham estate. Some 15 years later the figure had climbed to nearly 30,000 acres, though it was hiring much less. Subsequently, economic and social change took much of the wind out of the scheme's sails, and from the early 1960s it has been a story of steady retreat. Small concrete NCC marker posts can still be seen at a number of places in the countryside.

BUSES and LORRIES

The development of passenger carrying transport was boosted by a number of factors, including the sale of redundant First World War vehicles which could be adapted for hackney work, the railway strike of 1919, and the arrival from America of a light, pneumatic-tyred bus able to carry 14 to 20 passengers. The next five years was a story of unqualified success for the industry, however, for during that period the number of passenger vehicle licences climbed from 41,800 in 1918 to 82,800 in 1921.[27] By 1926 the number touched 100,000, and horse-drawn buses were a thing of the past. The spread of services to country districts was an important

new element, bringing
mobility into peoples'
lives. It also helped make
possible the spread of
towns and encouraged the
planning of garden suburbs
and ribbon development,
social changes which also
benefited from the
increasing popularity of
private cars just after the
First World War, and more
particularly, in the 1950s.
Lorries appeared on our
roads at the time of the
First World War, too,
many of the new haulage
contractors also buying
their vehicles cheaply in
military sell-offs. In turn,
increased lorry use forced
the new-formed Ministry

An Edward VII postbox at Tunstall.

of Transport to develop fresh policies on road planning and maintenance. In a
sense the haulage industry is forcing this again, if only because the number of
lorries seems to have increased in direct proportion to their size and bulk. Always
ahead of the field, they are once again too numerous and too large for many of the
local roads and lanes. A great deal of physical damage has already been done to
road surfaces and verge sides, and it is possible to find lorry battle scars in most
country lanes. The Norfolk Society, commenting on the issue,[90] said it can 'forsee
a situation where HGVs may have to get a permit to travel down country lanes.'
Weight and size restrictions will surely come.

STREET FURNITURE
Pillar and post boxes
They take their name from the Doric Pillar, and Norfolk can still boast some
Victorian mail boxes and at least one of King Edward V11. The oldest wall-box
in Norfolk is thought to be an 1861 example at Bramerton, while the oldest pillar
box in Norwich is that facing the market on the corner of The Walk and London
Street. It dates from between 1866 and 1879.

Signs clutter

Once upon a time we just had signposts, but now we also have direction signs, parking signs, speed limit signs, village signs, street and lane signs, brown Places of Interest signs, and sometimes village hall signs. The latest additions, at least in the countryside, are vast, disproportionately large village signs. Sometimes versions of them appear in clusters, producing a sort of visual garbage heap also attacked by The Norfolk Society.[90]

Non-plastic bollards

They were used to prevent coaches and carts from damaging nearby property, particularly near corners where the turning room was tight. Now they are used, mainly, to mark property boundaries and keep lorries at bay. Some in Cley are old ships' cannon.

Bridges

When Norfolk County Council was formed in 1888 it inherited some 267 bridges, a number which climbed even higher as more and more roads were adopted. Most distressingly, many of the bridges were crumbling, the timbers were rotting, and they were being shaken to bits by steam engines and the like. Slowly, they began a programme of re-building, repair or replacement, and most brick county bridges date from this 1890s to 1930s period.

Pavements

Until well into the 18th century discerning town dwellers placed planks and stones across streets to avoid having to walk in the mud. Remember, there was no civic lighting, no sewage system as we know it today, no street cleaning and no building regulations. Another way to avoid such muddy distress was to dump tons of flint cobbles in the slough to try to improve the surface. There is evidence this was done at Cley in 1738,[62] thanks to public subscription, and that vessels possibly loaded with flint cobbles brought 'paving stones' into the ports of Blakeney and Cley in the 1780s. Of 15 separate shipments in one year, four loads went to Wisbech, two to Spalding, six to Ipswich and one each to Boston, Gainsborough and Harwich. During the 1790s discussions[91] took place on how to improve pavements - presumably with flagstones - modernise bridges and introduce street lighting, and the ideas finally became reality in a series of Paving Acts. That for Norwich dates to 1806, Great Yarmouth 1810, and Wells 1844, but the earliest in Norfolk was at King's Lynn, dating between 1803 and 1806.

Redundant roads

When a road is replaced (by a bypass or ring road, for example) the land is hardly ever returned to nature, or to farming. Sometimes it is simply left and ignored, which is what has happened to a short stretch of the old A11 at Hargham Heath, south-west of Attleborough. Likewise when bends are straightened, the curved, redundant bits are often turned into laybys, a policy which can be seen, for example, at several places on the A47 in the vicinity of Swaffham and East Dereham. And thereby hangs another tale, for laybys have played an important role in our transport culture, and indeed, have become places in their own right, some of them offering rest, recreation and refreshment. Of course, there may have been other restorations, but the only piece of redundant road I can actually recall which has disappeared was a short section of a minor lane near a junction which once ran from Triangle Covert, East Harling, towards Middle Harling church. Talking of road improvements, did you know that some of the first road traffic accident studies were conducted in Oxfordshire and Lanarkshire between 1932 and 1936?[27] And do you know what the Lanarkshire study found? It concluded there were 80 per cent fewer accidents on dual carriageways than on single carriageway roads.

NATURE RESERVES
The entire 22 miles from Holme to Weybourne is designated as a Site of Special Scientific Interest, and it has a number of other world and European designations, too. In this context it is interesting to note that Norfolk Wildlife Trust (formally Norfolk Naturalists' Trust) was founded in 1926, making it the first county-based voluntary nature conservation body in the country, and that it currently has about 6500 acres of reserves. In fact the NWT is one of only a number of like-minded organisations represented in Norfolk, some of the others being the National Trust, the Royal Society for the Protection of Birds, National Nature Reserve and English Heritage. The list of nature reserves in the county is a long one, but it includes areas at Blakeney Point, Cley Marshes, East Winch Common, Foxley Wood, Holkham, Holt Lowes, Holme Dunes, Morston, Stiffkey, Salthouse Marsh, Scolt Head, Snettisham, Thursford Wood, Titchwell Marsh, Narborough (railway embankment), Ringstead Downs, Roydon Common, Syderstone Common, Ashwellthorpe Wood, Booton Common, Hethel (Old Thorn), Hoe Rough, Honeypot Wood, Sparham Pools, Wayland Wood, East Wretham Heath, New Buckenham Common, Thompson Common, Weeting Heath, Alderfen Broad, Berney Marshes, Breydon Water, Cockshoot Broad, Horsey Mere, Hickling Broad, Martham Broad, Strumpshaw Fen, Surlingham Church Marsh, and Upton Fen.

NEW-LOOK FARMING
Economically pressured arable farmers seem to be enduring another difficult period when it seems they want to be anything but arable farmers, converting their land into caravan parks and golf courses, or raising deer or ostrich. This followed an earlier phase when some of them were paid not to do certain things, such as not to run pigs on heathland. Now the new agricultural climate - which meteorological

experts warn will end in fields of sunflowers (or ice sheets) stretching as far as the eye can see - has turned in another direction, towards set-aside land. This is an ostensibly sensible scheme to take land out of production to avoid having to grow, and pay for, cereal crops which apparently no one wants. Set-aside fields, amid otherwise pristine farming landscapes, look unloved, uncared for and untidy. Presumably wildlife likes them, for some have been designated as nature areas. Other set-aside land has been planted with woodland, which is a considerable improvement on filling it with concrete and building bungalows, which presumably means (as with redundant roads) that this redundant land could never again be handed back to nature.

COLOURFUL COUNTRYSIDE

Walkers in the Norfolk countryside during the summer months, particularly, may see fields coloured brilliant yellow or pale blue. Assuming we are not talking about the cereal harvest, then the brilliant yellow crops will be either mustard, of which a little is still grown, or more likely the new kid on the block, oilseed rape, which is harvested to help make margarine and lubricating oil. The pale blue fields, which from afar can look like lakes, are either borage, or flax - particularly in the Gayton area, and only a few miles from the former flax processing factory at West Newton, where it was harvested from 1931 to 1955 - which is grown for linseed. Woad and camomile have also been recorded in the county. Here are a few more colourful plants:

Poppies
A wonderful sight in early summer. Some special poppies are grown under licence at 'secret locations' to provide seed for the medical and catering industries. But it is the wild, uncultivated varieties that lend such a welcoming blush to our verges and field edges. Once cut and sprayed to the very edge of depletion, poppies seem to be making something of a comeback. They love disturbed soil, and seed can lay dormant for a century before flowering when the ground is disturbed.[92] In turn, this has invested them with a symbolism of death and rebirth and, thanks to the bombs and shells of the First World War, an association with war. The poppy is a tough, resilient flower coming in several hues, which in the late 19th and early 20th centuries, and thanks to Clement Scott,[93] once gave Cromer and its immediate catchment area a flavour and character all of its own. I love to see them.

Rosebay willowherb
An extraordinary plant, this is what gives Breckland its pinkish tinge during the summer months. Rosebay was first recorded in 1597[50] but it has risen from relative obscurity to abundance during the last 150 years, and despite several theories no-one really knows why. Lowland rosebay may have been introduced into England from America or Central Europe in the 17th century, but in any event, by about

1840 it had reached half the counties of England. Its real chance seems to have arrived with the railways, for it relishes raw soil and quickly invades burned ground. The new rail earthworks aided seed transportation, and two wars and the ensuing disturbances encouraged even further growth. Now it decorates woodland and field fringes and in Breckland, at least, helps soften the plantation outlines.

Hawthorn

A plant full of symbolism and meaning, it is gorgeous in May and June, for it makes some hedgerow stretches, such as those alongside the Peddars Way near Bircham, look as if they have been liberally dusted with snow. It is our most common hedgerow plant and its name means 'hedge thorn.' Its blossom is said to herald the arrival of summer, and is thus known as 'May,' and for generations has been associated with maypole ceremonies. Hawthorn also features in early ecclesiastical symbolism and carving, while its crimson haws are part of England's traditional autumn scene.

Cow-parsley

Not on everyone's list of favourite countryside plants, cow-parsley nevertheless lends a certain frothy white delicacy to the fringes of hedges, cemeteries, rough field boundaries, and many roadside verges, and is very common in the countryside. In south Lincolnshire, in my youth, we called it 'keck,' for reasons which escaped me, but I see that its posh name is Kex Anthriscus Sylvestris, so we nearly got it right. Oliver Rackham,[50] in discussing churchyards, made the point that 'the nettle and cow-parsley are a memento mori, for in them is recycled, while awaiting the Last Trump, part of the phosphate of 10,000 skeletons.' Makes you think, that.

Broom and gorse/furze

Common on heathland, they can set the edges of some of Breckland's forest rides ablaze with golden yellow, particularly in May and early June. They are under shrubs, known from the 4th century, which adore sunshine. If burned or cut in youth or middle age they simply sprout from the base like coppicing trees. Furze, in fact, was an important fuel, for it is said to burn with a hot blaze and is therefore particularly suitable for ovens. English and Norse place-names alluding to broom, bracken and furze included brom, whin and ling, which in turn may have led to Brampton, Bracondale and Whinburgh.

Third Age Walkers

This section is aimed specifically at those who have often thought of taking up leisure walking but are reluctant to make the first step, or maybe think they are no longer up to the task; and at those who perhaps already enjoy a stroll and are beginning to turn over in their mind the idea of upgrading to something a little longer. In other words, and in general terms, the over-50s. Of course, some will point out that Norfolk is not ranked among the top counties for footpaths, but do not use that as an excuse. Even in Norfolk, in 1991[112] anyway, there were said to be 2250 miles of paths. There is ample scope.

THE REASONS WHY

Let me dispose of the two most oft-posed questions right at the start: (1) Am I too old to begin leisure walking? No. And (2) could I actually complete a long distance walk? Yes. It is as simple as that. Or rather, it is all about planning a walk in such a way that you are able to complete it with maximum ease and minimum discomfort.

It is a tiny matter of personal regret that I was 38 when I began, thus missing out on more athletic years when I might - in theory, at least - have tackled Scotland's mountains, Lakeland's hills, Cornwall's cliffs, or even the lonely expanses of the Pennine Way. Nevertheless, I was suddenly pitched into a 50-mile walk along the Peddars Way during a week-long heatwave with no real knowledge of how to do it and little proper equipment. That my companion and I did reach Holme and the coast, albeit in such a state of exhaustion we had to be 'rescued' by our families, I have always interpreted as a somewhat extraordinary event. In that light, and given that my feet took six weeks to heal, the fact that I have elected to do something similar every year since then might be interpreted as a minor miracle. To be brutally honest, although a stroll or a day's walk is undeniably enjoyable, a walk of five, six or seven days with a rucksack on your back is an experience of a quite different dimension. Having long since given up tenting, wading across the Little Ouse or the Thet rivers, sleeping beside hedges or in fields, and trying to cook in the rain or wash in cattle troughs, the last few years have been devoted to the rather more satisfying occupation of trying to make such walks as relaxing as possible.

In one sense we have forgotten a good deal of the art of walking, for what might now seem a prodigious distance was once the norm, and more, was completed without fuss or fancy kit. There are innumerable examples in literature. Thomas Hardy's characters regularly walked 15 miles to town or market and then walked home again. Gypsy Gordon Boswell[83] recounted how, in 1907 at the age of 12, he walked from Doddington, in Cambridgeshire, all the way to Lowestoft and back again; and from Doddington to King's Lynn and on to Hunstanton and Heacham, where his pal was looking after the bathing machines on the beach; and so on. And in 1833 George Borrow, seeking a job interview with the Foreign Bible Society and with precious little money, walked the 112 miles from Norwich to London in 27 hours, stopping only for bread, milk, beer and apples. On the other hand Harriet Martineau's biographer[94] records that in 1845/46 the great lady lived near Ambleside not far from the poet Wordsworth, then 76, with whom she was on neighbourly, even close terms. Harriet and William were both habitual strollers, but William's sister Dorothy, later the writer Dorothy Quillinan, 'had not once but frequently walked 40 miles a day.' And I recall, in attempting to explain my tiredness, proudly telling a relation how the previous day I had completed the 23-mile Forest Walk from West Stow to Didlington. He promptly recounted how, as a boy, he had walked from Sheringham to Norwich, attended the cattle

The Roman soldiery used tents, evidently made of leather, but it was not until the late 18th century, and because of the cost of staying at an inn, that other travellers contemplated using them. One of the earliest recorded 'tourists' to have carried a tent was Thomas De Quincey. Using a contraption 'not larger than an ordinary umbrella,' which he made from canvas, De Quincey was adept[105] at 'sleeping among the ferns or furze upon a hillside.' Many 18th and 19th century walkers seem to have largely ignored the possibility of getting wet, accepting it was part and parcel of the pastime. Occasionally a walker carried an umbrella, but the usual trick was to dry off overnight in front of a landlady's fire, or simply sleep in damp clothes. Not until the widespread availability of waterproof clothing, it seems, did we develop a distaste for walking in the rain.

market, and then walked back to Sheringham accompanied by and in the sole charge of five head of cattle.

Of course, four of the five examples mentioned above walked to market, to London, Heacham or to Sheringham because they had to. There were few other alternatives. We, on the other hand, just like Harriet, William and Dorothy, and over short or long distances, tend to walk for pleasure and exercise. If asked to explain why, I would have to say there is a very particular kind of freedom attached to it, a sort of refreshment which is not obtainable in any other way, and a psychological pull which, come what may, reasserts itself each January or February and possesses the mind until a spring or summer week is finally designated and marked on the calendar and the next walk organised. But be warned. In advocating a case for a Ramblers' Anonymous organisation, Mike Harding[104] pointed out: 'Weaning the addict from his dependence is a slow and painful process.'

Two occurrences largely shaped the outline of this book, and this section in particular. One was the realisation that an above average number of walkers who enjoy the Peddars Way and Norwich Coast Path are past the first blush of youth and are either retired or close to retirement. I am sure there are a number of reasons for this (a fairly comfortable terrain, good pubs and beer, fish and chips in Blakeney, bird-watching, etc), but the fact remains that for a great many people this particular local long distance trail, as it was for me, is an excellent proving ground, a relatively user-friendly walk for mature first-timers. In fact, if I may add a further note of sobriety, recent research[113] suggested that the average

There have been many euphemisms for walking, yomp being a relatively recent addition to the list. For a long time walkers were unpopular, largely because it was assumed they simply could not afford to ride. Later, when walking became fashionable, it was thought the lower classes would not be any good at it because of poor diet and a consequent lack of stamina. Then when it did become fashionable a 'language' was introduced to disguise the fact that it actually meant walking, including words such as 'peripatetics' (17th century), 'post-jentacular circumgyrations' (18th century), 'the grinds' (Oxford/Cambridge, 18th century), and 'constitutional,' (18th and 19th century). In 1856 the Prince of Wales, then 14, was taken on a walking tour of Dorset under orders to avoid 'a slouching gait with hands in pockets.'

walker on our National Trail is probably male and aged between 45 and 59. Moreover, his reasons for walking it are (a) scenery and landscape, (b) nature, and (c) peace and quiet. The other occurrence was a chance meeting in Overy Staithe a couple of years ago with a group of walkers. They were all from Leicestershire, none had been on a long distance walk before, and they were on a walking holiday because they had all taken early retirement. Twenty years ago they might have stayed at home and watched telly. Instead, they were exploring new territory and enjoying the fresh air. So can you. Do it.

Footpath sign and major landmark, near Swardeston.

THE BIG CIRCLE

Any decent Norfolk bookshop is stuffed with titles about local walks, or at least has a foot or two of shelving devoted to the subject. There are walk books large and small, pamphlets and maps, books on straight walks, curved walks, walks from pubs and walks back to pubs, circular walks from straight walks, historical walks, and walks that don't seem to do anything. In fact, there is something to suit every requirement. Thus you do not require similar information from me. However, I will mention the Forest Walk (details from the Forestry Commission at Santon Downham) which is a long day's yomp, about 23 miles, and can be walked either when there is no one else on the paths or on the one day a year, usually in April, when it is highly organised and when hundreds take part, most of them raising money for a multitude of good causes. The Icknield Way (Ivinghoe Beacon to Knettishall), the Nar Valley Way (King's Lynn to Gressenhall), the Wash Way

A group of walkers near Swardeston.

(Sutton Bridge to Lynn) and Boudica's Way (Norwich to Diss) are also worth contemplating.

Incidentally, most of walk titles are based on the assumption that a car and a parking space need to be available nearby while the routes themselves need to be in the three to 10-mile category. This is understandable, so you have to search the shelves a little more diligently if you have your heart set on a local walk of several days, or even a week. On the other hand, impromptu, 'unofficial' walks are always possible if you like inventing your own, if you are good at reading maps and like walking the lanes, and if you can find either camping sites (if tenting) or bed and breakfast establishments (if not). My second long walk was east to west across Norfolk, but it involved a lot of time-wasting diversions and an above average amount of road walking. If you prefer a more comfortable ratio of paths and waymarks and a higher level of organisation, then there are four routes available: the Peddars Way (Knettishall to Holme, circa 46 miles), the Norfolk Coast Path (Hunstanton to Cromer, circa 49 miles), the Weavers' Way (Cromer to Great Yarmouth, circa 57 miles), and the Angles Way (Great Yarmouth to Knettishall, circa 77 miles), which together constitute a circa 230-mile route in a rough circle all the way round the county.

Usually, the Peddars Way and Coast Path are lumped together because they represent an official Countryside Commission national long distance trail of some 93/96 miles (the length irregularity is because of route variations and local choices) and because a single guidebook[95] deals with both. Similarly, the Weavers' and Angles Way routes are also dealt with in a single guidebook.[96] For anyone contemplating walking any of them I would also recommend three other publications, a Norfolk County Council leaflet on the Weavers' Way,[97] an historical description of the landscape through which the Angles Way passes,[98] and a transport and accommodation guide to the Peddars Way and Coast Path,[99] updated and published annually by the Ramblers' Association. All these paths are suitable for beginners or older walkers, the Coast Path perhaps being the easiest simply because it has more facilities (ie, shops, transport, accommodation) to offer. If you are contemplating taking the plunge and walking the entire Grand Circle (meaning all four walks) in one go, then based on an average of 14 miles a day (see Walk Planning: Accommodation), and building in at least four rest days, the enterprise might take some 21 days and cost (see Walk Planning: Cost) in the region of £750.

WALK PLANNING
Route and timing
If you are toying with the idea of a first major walk then a week (which can mean seven walking days) is a good block of time. Anything longer than a week and terminal weariness can set in. The three long Norfolk walks mentioned above (Peddars/Coast, Weavers and Angles) can each be completed in that time, and in the end it boils down to a matter of geographical preference and the best places to arrange start/finish transport. For example, whereas Knettishall, Hunstanton and Holme require either car or bus connection, Cromer and Yarmouth can at least be reached from Norwich by rail. Of the four routes, the Peddars Way and Coast Path trail (which you can treat as one walk) has the most variety, the Weavers' Way is the easiest, while the Angles Way is in some ways the prettiest. As for time of year, the winter means you take pot luck with the weather, while during the peak summer months it can be very crowded along the coastline. My own preference is for the early weeks of June, before the holiday season has reached its climax and while the vegetation is still green and fresh.
Accommodation
You need to decide an ideal average daily walking distance which, according to experience and health, might be anywhere between 10 and 30 miles. In 1934 Arthur Sharp[106] recommended 12 to 15 miles a day for the average tramper. Let us assume the magic figure is 14 (which happens to be my magic figure). If you

A Federation of Rambling Clubs was founded in 1905 by Sir Lawrence Chubb and Mr JA Southern. Other federations also sprang into being, but they all came together in 1931 to create the National Council of Rambling Federations. In 1935 this in turn became the Ramblers Association. Norfolks national trail, the Peddars Way and Coast Path, came into being on July 8, 1986, when it was opened by HRH The Prince of Wales at a public ceremony on the beach at Holme. A voluntary organisation, the Peddars Way Association, subsequently wound up, was founded in November, 1981, to help oversee the establishment of the trail, create interest in it, and collate a walkers accommodation list.

have chosen to walk the circa 96-mile Peddars Way and Coast Path trail, then 96 divided by 14 gives you, roughly, a seven-day walk. So, and assuming you are not tenting, with your maps on one side and an accommodation guide[99] on the other, you can now start looking for bed and breakfast establishments roughly 14 miles apart. And this is where you hit the first snag. Only rarely are they 14 miles apart. Thus one of your days might be only 11 miles, another 16 or 17. You have to fit them in as best you can, taking into account the difficulty or otherwise of the terrain. Three other points. First, B&Bs can be relatively scarce in some inland areas but generally plentiful along the coast. Second, if you are planning your walk during the summer it is necessary to book accommodation well in advance. Never assume you can start looking for a B&B at 4pm after a long day's walk; you might end up sleeping under a hedge. And third, whereas there used to be some resistance, most B&B landladies no longer slam the door if they see you have muddy boots and dripping clothes. Nowadays, most of them are helpfulness personified.

Cost

Oddly, walking is no longer particularly cheap unless you take a tent and live off the land. At the time of writing the cost of B&Bs in Norfolk is edging towards £20 a night; then, and aside from any start/finish transport costs, you must also take into account the need to buy refreshments and bits and pieces along the way and, most importantly, a substantial meal every evening. As a rule of thumb guide, and purely on 1998 prices, calculate on needing at least £35 a day.

What to carry

This is a personal matter, but there is a self-evident need for a good pair of boots or sturdy, water-proof shoes, a good set of lightweight rain wear, and a water-proof rucksack, preferably with lots of outside pockets. You might also need maps, or a guidebook, and a map case. Other essentials are a toilet bag; spare insoles, trousers, socks and underclothes; warm shirts or a top; a sweater; a pair of shoes/trainers; something to wear in the evenings; a small medical kit (plasters, nail scissors, Germolene, sting treatment); a small (possibly plastic) bottle of water/drink, and a bite or two to eat (fruit, sandwiches, nuts and raisins or, if the weather is not too hot, chocolate). I also carry a black plastic bin liner - useful for putting things in or sitting on if the grass it wet - a small towel, and a drop of scotch, otherwise known as Foot Lotion. Pack spare things at the bottom, bad weather clothing towards the top, and when you have finished pop the filled rucksack on to the bathroom scales. If it indicates 25lb or above, empty it, throw some things away, and try again.

DAY WALKS
Or even part-day walks, of course, which can be anything from three to 10 miles or more, and preferably circular, to bring you back to your car particularly in rural areas where public transport may be a trifle thin on the ground. Again, lightweight rain wear is essential, together with a small day pack, a little drink and perhaps a bite to eat. Stop and take regular 10-minute rests (as outlined below) before you become fatigued.

LONG WALK ROUTINE
On week-long walks it is important to avoid fatigue as much as possible, so design your daily programme as a series of short walks with short rests between. A sensible programme might be 45 or 60 minutes' walking followed by a 10-minute rest. Decide what is best for you, and stick to your plan. Have a good breakfast and a good meal in the evening. At lunch time, on the trail, it is wise to have a drink (water, fruit juice) and a bite or two to eat, something to give you energy but not fill you up. I usually get by with an apple, a stick of flapjack or a bar of chocolate. Also during the lunch stop, take off your boots to air them, and change your socks over. It helps to prevent chafing. Change your boot insoles every two or three days.
Tender subject
Arthur Sharp[106] recommended bathing the feet, pre-walk, in salt water to harden them and then rubbing them with Vaseline before putting on your boots. I once tried a lengthy pre-walk course of surgical spirit, which seemed to work even though the smell was awful. More recently I have not bothered, preferring to be more responsive to chafing while actually on the walk. I have my own remedies. Sore spots: cover immediately with Germolene. Raw spots: plaster immediately,

but remember to take the plaster off at night to enable it to begin healing. Blisters: burst, plaster, uncover at night.

HOME TRUTHS

Never dither about the weather. If you are properly equipped, and providing conditions are not extreme: Go.

The faster the rain, the quicker it stops.

Other warnings of rain or unsettled weather, according to Arthur Sharp,[106] include sheep with their tails to windward; cows stretching their necks or shifting uneasily under trees; horses galloping up and down; and rabbits feeding in the afternoon, which indicates rain in the evening.

Another way of telling what the weather has in store is to look into the wind and see what the sky is blowing in.

Beware changeable weather near the sea. The coastline can have its own micro climate which is often quite different to the weather further inland.

Remember that miles walked before lunch are worth more than those walked afterwards, so a good start in the morning is a positive advantage.

Do not adopt someone else's stride pattern. Walk at your own pace.

Unless you walk alone, try to have an even number in your group, for an odd number can introduce an element of difficulty. An odd number often means one walker being on his/her own, and there can be problems in finding accommodation. Few B&Bs can accommodate a single, whereas nearly all have twin-bedded rooms.

If buckles, straps, socks or laces start bothering you, put them right immediately. In other words, treat sore places as soon as you become aware of them, not at the end of the day.

Stop and rest BEFORE you start to feel tired.

Stick to your walking programme (for example, 45 minutes' walking, 10 minutes' rest) and try to pace yourself.

If you must think about the distance scheduled for the day, think about it in total, not about how many miles to go to the lunch stop.

It is a little known fact that boots and legs become inexplicably heavier as the day goes on; it follows, therefore, that stiles are harder to climb in the afternoon than in the morning.

If uphill walking tires you, shorten your stride, take it very slowly, try not to lose breath, and stop now and again to rest and to look around. In certain circles this is known as 'admiring the view.'

If thirsty on route, drink water or fruit juice. Lay off the beer until evening, particularly if the weather is hot. It can make you ill.

If uncertain which route alternative to take (for example, if a waymark has disappeared at a fork in the path), the first option is to re-check your map; the second is to check which path has the most footprints and is therefore the most widely used; while a third is to follow your own directional instinct.

If heat or tiredness overcome you, find shade or somewhere comfortable to sit; sleep or rest as long as necessary (remembering to stretch your legs occasionally, otherwise they may stiffen); and have a small amount to eat (if necessary) and a good

Church and lychgate at Hackford, near Hingham.

drink of water or fruit juice. Indeed, always make sure you have a good liquid intake. If painful feet or serious exhaustion overcome you, also consider the Foot Lotion option (see Helps).

On a long distance walk the second day is often worse - if you suffer from Sore Foot Syndrome - than the first. By the fourth day your feet should have hardened and you should be taking most things in your stride.

HELPS

Grass, hedges, trees, church porches, lich-gates, plastic bags
Despite the fact that lich (or lych) gates are otherwise known as corpse-gates, or as the place where priest and cortege can seek momentary shelter from the rain, this group represents the walkers' comfort zone, for they can all be used (a) as protection from inclement weather or (b) somewhere or something to sit under or on.

Water taps
In some places public taps are in short supply. For example, the only one I can think of on the Norfolk stretch of the Peddars Way is at Holme. Thus to find one

An unconcerned herd at Felbrigg.

on a hot day is bliss, enabling one to drink, re-fill liquid containers, and generally refresh one's-self. Most pub landlords are happy to fill your bottle, providing you also buy a beer or some crisps. In an emergency, cattle troughs can be pressed into service for washing, though not for drinking, providing you can operate the ball cock to get the water flowing.

Waymarks, maps, walks in newspapers and magazines
This group is included in the Helps section though they should all be treated with a degree of suspicion. Waymarks can be altered by fun-loving local youths, maps can prove confusing, and published walk instructions can be economical with the truth or abbreviated by space concious sub-editors. In an ideal world everything should work perfectly, but this group is the best we've got. Anyway, they add to the fun.

B&B breakfasts
Unless you have made prior arrangements, or the landlady is unusually adaptable, the breakfast will invariably be large and fried. Make full use of it, because this is an enormous help on a long walk as it means you can put off another proper meal until evening and require only a meagre bite at lunch time. The danger is that after a seventh fried breakfast in a row the system starts to pall. Still, you'll walk it off.

Pubs
Absolutely.

Pool, pooh-sticks

Two time-honoured games played by walkers. Pool is poor man's snooker and has the added advantage that you can complete three frames during a 30-minute stop. If you add each day's winning frames together you can end up with a 26-17 score at the end of a long walk. Pooh-sticks (where you drop sticks from a bridge into fast flowing water and then rush to the other side of the bridge to see whose stick appears first) can be a tense business unless you reach early agreement on the size and weight of the sticks and nominate a neutral bystander as starter.

Germolene, foot lotion

To paraphrase a well-known line from a famous film, I love the smell of Germolene in the morning. Excellent for cuts, bumps and sores, it has the added advantage that it can be massaged straight on to the feet. Foot Lotion (in reality any decent cooking whisky) can ease the pain of blisters. And a thimble-full a day can help to keep tiredness at bay.

Views to admire

Usually to be found in the vicinity of uphill slopes or rough terrain but, as mentioned earlier (see Home Truths), in an emergency almost any view can be turned into a fascinating panorama which simply shouts at you to pause and admire it.

Fellow walkers

No yomp would be the same without them. See also, Hazards.

HAZARDS

Mud, rain, wind, cold

You will almost certainly get some, so at least try to enjoy them.

Morning dew, heat, ruts, shingle, stones, dog dirt, kilometres

All of them are in the category of irritations. Dew can be surprisingly wet; heat very exhausting; shingle and stones punishing (it is best to find a more comfortable surface); dog dirt (decide which patch of grass you want to sit on, then you will find some) offensive; while kilometres are merely incomprehensible and unEnglish. Avoid them all, if possible.

Nettles, thistles, prickles, barbed wire

More than minor irritations, these are most usually associated with verges and field edges. Again, avoid if possible.

Traffic, tiredness

Fatigue in all its many guises is to be avoided if at all possible (see Views to Admire). Traffic is useful for getting to the start of walks and for getting home afterwards. Otherwise, treat with appropriate disdain.

Cattle, horses, dogs

Cattle and horses either wander away disinterestedly or cluster round you in fascinated groups. Sometimes they cluster so closely they will actually nudge you or try to investigate your pockets. If you are crossing an area inhabited by cattle or horses and are uncertain of the reception, or if some of the walking group are nervous of them, it is best to get into a close knot and walk slowly but straightforwardly in the direction you need to go. Another way, if the animals are determined to follow, is for one brave member of the group to wander off and lure the creatures away while the main group crosses to the fence or stile. Either way, stay calm, move slowly and deliberately, and do not make any sudden gestures or noises. If you meet a horse and rider in a narrow lane or on a bridleway, and particularly if the horse and/or rider seem young, it is best to step on to the verge, stand still, and let them pass you. Angry dogs present a different problem altogether. If corralled by a ferocious hound it is sometimes necessary to try to decide how angry/perplexed the creature really is. It is sometimes possible to quieten it simply by stopping, standing still, and speaking in soothing tones. If a dog appears very aggressive I have occasionally found that the reason seems to be the outline made by my rucksack. So another way to try to quieten it is to stop, take off your rucksack, place it on the ground, and talk gently. On no account offer a hand. It might decide to accept.

Rabbits, flies, insects, ants

Some walkers carry cans of insect repellent, but it can sometimes mean doing an uneconomic amount of spraying. Much better to move out of the way, into the sunlight or into the open. Check all ground for ants before sitting down. Rabbits are not a problem unless you see some lying or staggering about in the undergrowth. In Norfolk, particularly if their eyes are swollen and they are dying of disease or starvation, then they have probably got myxomatosis, a ghastly man-made rabbit hell. Alas, there is nothing you can do for them.

Farmers, crops

Farmers automatically assume each and every walker is about to distribute tons of litter, pick up and carry off the fertiliser bags he has carefully left blowing about, leave gates open to allow his animals to escape, destroy his privacy, disturb his pheasants, tread on his crops and wreck his machinery. Perhaps some do. Most ramblers, however, simply want to walk the public rights of away and enjoy the open air. Not many farmers (placed by Mike Harding[104] in the category agricolus manicus) understand this, so in general terms it is best to give them a wide berth. On the other hand you do have rights, so if a public right of way has been ploughed, cropped or obstructed - and one survey[114] suggested that 75 per cent of paths crossing arable fields were difficult or impossible to follow - walk through the crop. Nicely, of course, on the correct route, and between the rows. The official line from the Countryside Commission[115] is that you are allowed to take a short detour round an illegal obstruction, or remove it sufficiently to get past.

Assorted ailments

Mike Harding[104] has identified stile crotch, electric fence tear duct, tea bloat, wet grass bum rot and bull phobia as key hazards. Most regular walkers will be familiar with them.

Sore feet, blisters

See Walk Routine: Tender subject (above). The big philosophical debate was always, and still is for that matter, the contentious question of the bursting or non-bursting of blisters. It is a very personal thing. After extensive trials I can only say that the answer for me (though not for everyone) is: first burst, then plaster; plaster off at night to give it air. The best answer to every foot problem is to try to avoid them in the first place.

Where the Peddars Way crosses the Heacham River at Fring Cross.

Fellow walkers

See also, Helps: Fellow walkers. Some can be too slow, others too fast. A few are always late or excessively noisy or untidy. Some talk too much, or grumble, while others want to be left alone. Also, if you have an odd number it is difficult to arrange the pub pool games short of organising a league. Nurture with care.

LEGALLY SPEAKING

There are about 120,000 miles of rights of way in England, and local government authorities are required to keep maps of them and to inform Ordnance Survey. A highway authoritity (which often owns the path, but not necessarily the soil beneath) also has a duty to signpost a right of way where it leaves a metalled road.

All rights of way (other than public highways) fall into four categories - footpaths, bridleways, byways open to all traffic, and roads used as public paths. But the matter is greatly complicated. A green lane or canal towpath, for example, can be any one of the four. A fifth category embraces 'permissive' paths, and relies on the goodwill of the land owner.[117][118]

Rights of way

Fully opened rights of way, which include the first four categories mentioned above, grant the public specified rights of access providing they behave responsibly. You may pass with a pram, pushchair or wheelchair, if practicable, and carry any items connected with 'your immediate recreation,' meaning cameras, binoculars, sketching materials, etc. You may also sit by the side of a right of way to rest, eat a simple picnic, take a photograph or sketch. Any act which is not a reasonable part of the journey risks prosecution under the trespass laws.

Land owners

They are restricted on what they can do with footpaths. They may not plough or disturb any footpath or bridleway which runs around the edge of a field, or disturb any byway at all. They are allowed to plough up any footpath or bridleway which runs across a field, and even cultivate or harvest a crop on it, but they must make it clear to the public where the line of the path remains, and they must restore it within 24 hours of any disturbance or two weeks of the disturbance if a crop is being planted. The highway authority can prosecute an offending farmer, or charge for remedial work.

User responsibility

Dogs must be kept under close control, and some local bye-laws may prevent dog fouling. Flora and fauna must be protected. It is an offence to leave litter.

Bulls

Bulls are allowed provided they are under 11 months old and do not belong to any of the recognised dairy herds (Ayrshire, British Friesian or Holstein, Dairy Shorthorn, Guernsey, Jersey or Kerry). Other bulls are banned unless accompanied by cows or heifers. But farmers or land owners may be held responsible for injuries caused by grazing animals if aware of a risk.

Footpaths

There are about 90,000 miles of them in England, and they may be used only for walking.

Bridleways

Walkers still have a priority, but bridleways may also be used for riding or leading a horse, donkey or mule. Cyclists (including mountain bikers) are allowed, though they must give way to other users. Other vehicles, motorised or horse-drawn, are banned. There are about 25,000 miles of them in England.

Byways open to all traffic
In effect they are minor roads, usually unmetalled, which anyone can use.
Roads used as public paths
The legal definition is complex but they offer the same rights as bridleways, plus, in some cases, vehicles.
Open country, common land
All common land is owned, by an individual, company or local authority. The public has access to common land in urban areas; elsewhere, commons have legal public access if special agreements or Acts have been made.

On the trail: Halvergate.

LAST WORDS
At the time of writing the many issues affecting the countryside stand in grave danger of becoming locked into a Them versus Us argument, fashioned into a sort of war between apparently diverging Rural and Urban politics, strategies and opinions. In truth, of course, the issues need to be seen not as those of division but as parts of the whole. In much the same way the countryside also needs to be seen as a delicate balancing act between those who work in or manage it and those who simply want to enjoy it. Essentially, the countryside belongs to all sides of the divide. At the same time, and from the standpoint of walkers, it is also clear that changes are afoot, ranging from a political debate over voluntary access agreements and potential 'right to roam' legislation,[119] to suggestions of rural 'tranquil zones' where cars would give way to pedestrians.[120] We also need to appreciate that the countryside is an evolving history and natural history lesson which teaches us that over the centuries it has been constantly re-shaped by changing influences and circumstance. The countryside we see today is not traditional, because there is no

such thing as traditional; today's countryside is different to that of the 1940s, just as the 1940s countryside was different to the countryside of the 1790s. So we must not expect to be able to freeze landscape areas, or make habitats stand still, or even be frightened of evolutionary change. What should frighten us more is the sort of loss of diversity and semi-permanent destruction most obviously introduced by concrete or by agricultural or industrial poisons, both of which do damage which even nature struggles to overcome and render safe.

By and large this has been a book about communications, and I ought to end it by looking forward to some of the next trends. Frankly, and once again, the future is obscure. No more major road building programmes, perhaps? Increased costs and further restrictions on motor vehicles? An expansion of park and ride schemes? A brief, new burgeoning of local railway services? A 1920s-style bus revival? Cycling as fashionable in Norwich as it is in Amsterdam? We shall see. The one certainty is that there will still be walkers. What we need to ensure is that there will still be somewhere to walk.

REFERENCES AND BIBLIOGRAPHY

1. Brewer's Dictionary of Phrase & Fable. Book Club Associates, 1985.
2. The Road Goes On. CW Scott-Giles, The Epworth Press, 1948.
3. The Old Road. Hilaire Belloc, Constable, 1911.
4. The Icknield Way. Edward Thomas, Constable, 1916; re-issued Wildwood House, 1980.
5. The English Path. Kim Taplin, Boydell, 1979.
6. The Open Air. Richard Jefferies, The Wayfarer's Library, undated.
7. The Traveller's Quotation Book. Edited by Jennifer Taylor, Hale, 1993.
8. The Roadmender. Michael Fairless, Duckworth, 1902; re-issued Wildwood House, 1981.
9. Norfolk Origins: 1 Hunters to First Farmers. Bruce Robinson, Acorn Editions, 1981.
10. An Historical Atlas of Norfolk. Edited by Peter Wade-Martins, Norfolk Museums Service, 1993.
11. A Festival of Norfolk Archaeology. Edited by Margeson, Ayers & Heywood, Norfolk & Norwich Archaeological Society, 1996.
12. The Origins of Norfolk. Tom Williamson, Manchester University Press, 1993.
13. Current Archaeology, No 153, Vol 13, No 9. June, 1997.
14. The European newspaper. June 26, 1993.
15. A History of Thetford. Alan Crosby, Phillimore, 1986.
16. Norfolk Origins: 2 Roads & Tracks. Robinson & Rose, Poppyland, 1983.
17. The Quarterly, No 14. Journal of the Norfolk Archaeological and Historical Research Group, 1994.
18. British Archaeology, No 20. Council for British Archaeology, 1996.
19. Chasing the Shadows: Norfolk Mysteries Revisited. Bruce Robinson, Elmstead Publications, 1996.
20. Roman Roads. Raymond Chevallier, Batsford, 1989.
21. Roman Britain: a sourcebook, 2nd edtn. S Ireland, Routledge, 1996.
22. Medieval Roads. Brian Hindle, Shire Archaeology, 1982.
23. Travellers in Britain. Richard Trench, Aurum, 1990.
24. Travel in England. Thomas Burke, Scribner, 1946.
25. Norfolk Origins: 4 The North Folk. Bond, Penn & Rogerson, Poppyland, 1990.
26. Norfolk Origins: 3 Celtic Fire & Roman Rule. Robinson & Gregory, Poppyland, 1987.
27. British Roads. Geoffrey Boumphrey, Nelson, 1939.

28. The Old Roads of England. Sir William Addison, Batsford, 1980.
29. England. HV Morton, Book Club Associates, 1975.
30. An Elizabethan Progress. Zillah Dovey, Sutton, 1996.
31. The Domesday Book. Edited by Thomas Hinde, Coombe, 1996.
32. The Norfolk Landscape. David Dymond, Hodder & Stoughton, 1985.
33. Norfolk Origins: 5 Deserted Villages in Norfolk. Alan Davison, Poppyland, 1996.
34. Faden's Map of Norfolk. The Lark's Press, 1989.
35. The Batsford Companion to Local History. Stephen Friar, Batsford, 1991.
36. The Norfolk Broads: a landscape history. Tom Williamson, Manchester University Press, 1997.
37. A Social History of England. Asa Briggs, BCA, 1994.
38. The King's Highway. Rees Jeffreys, Batchworth, 1949.
39. Eastern Daily Press: 100 Years Ago. May 6, 1997.
40. Eastern Daily Press: 100 Years Ago. January 22, 1997.
41. The Stoke Ferry Turnpike. J F Fone, article, Norfolk Archaeology, vol 38, pt 2. Norfolk & Norwich Archaeological Society, 1982.
42. Centenary: 100 Years of County Government in Norfolk. Edited by Clive Wilkins-Jones. Norfolk County Council Libraries & Information Service, 1989.
43. A History of Roads. Geoffrey Hindley, Citadel, 1972.
44. The Concise Oxford Dictionary of English Place-names, 4th edition. Eilert Ekwall, Clarendon, 1981.
45. The Alignment of Norfolk's Peddars Way in Relation to Natural Watercourses. Bruce Robinson, essay, 1997, unpublished.
46. Ribbons from the Pedlar's Pack. Ben Ripper, Ripper, 1979.
47. Collins Field Guide to Archaeology in Britain. Eric Wood, Collins, 1973.
48. Ley Lines in Question. Williamson & Bellamy, World's Work, 1983.
49. The Placing of Stones. Alan Davison, article, The Quarterly, No 2, Norfolk Archaeological and Historical Research Group, 1996.
50. A History of the Countryside. Oliver Rackham, Dent, 1986.
51. Fields, Tracks and Boundaries in the Creakes, North Norfolk. Mary Hesse, article, Norfolk Archaeology, vol XLI, pt 3. Norfolk and Norwich Archaeological Society, 1992.
52. The Guardian, Education section. June 13, 1995.
53. Norwich Bridges Past & Present. Cocke & Hall, The Norwich Society, 1994.
54. Shrines and Sacrifice. Ann Woodward, English Heritage/Batsford, 1992.
55. A History of Norfolk. Susanna Wade-Martins, Phillimore, 1984.
56. The Ruined and Disused Churches of Norfolk. Neil Batcock, East Anglian Archaeology 51, Norfolk Archaeological Unit, 1991.

57. Highway to Walsingham. Rev L Whatmore, Walsingham Pilgrim Bureau, 1973.
58. Monasteries of Norfolk. Richard Le Strange, Yates, 1973.
59. Inns and Inn Signs of Norfolk and Suffolk. Alfred Hedges, Circada, 1976.
60. Eastern Daily Press. September 25, 1993.
61. Historic Towns: Norwich. James Campbell, Scholar Press, 1975.
62. The Glaven Ports. Jonathan Hooten, Blakeney History Group, 1996.
63. A Popular Guide to Norfolk Place-names. James Rye, The Lark's Press, 1991.
64. The East Wind. Jane Hales, Veal, 1972.
65. Christopher Barringer, article. Eastern Daily Press, December 12, 1990.
66. Andy Reid, article. Norfolk Research Committee Bulletin, No 32, September, 1984.
67. One-inch Ordnance Survey map, sheet 46, first edition reprint. David & Charles, 1980.
68. Charles Roberts, article. Eastern Daily Press Magazine, October 25, 1997.
69. Milestones in Norfolk. Carol Haines, article, The Quarterly, No 24, Norfolk Archaeological and Historical Research Group, 1996.
70. Norwich Inns. Leonard Thompson, Harrison, 1947.
71. Bedlam. Huon Mallalieu, article. The Oldie magazine, No 104, November, 1997.
72. The Diary of a Country Parson, 1758-1802. James Woodforde, Oxford University Press, 1972.
73. History of Long Sutton & District. Robinson & Robinson, Long Sutton Civic Trust, 1981.
74. Heaths, Highwaymen and Gallows. Alan Davison, article, NARG News No 23, Norfolk Archaeological Rescue Group, 1980.
75. Tom Paine. John Keane, Bloomsbury, 1995.
76. St Faith's Fair, pts 1 & 2. Julian Eve, articles, The Quarterly, Nos 6 & 7, Norfolk Archaeological and Historical Research Group, 1992.
77. Eastern Daily Press. August 15, 1997.
78. If Stones Could Speak. RH Mottram, Museum Press, 1953.
79. Attleborough. Philip Bujak, Poppyland, 1990.
80. White's 1845 Directory. David & Charles reprint, 1969.
81. Green Lanes: report to the Countryside Commission. Dartington Amenity Research Trust, June, 1979.
82. In Breckland Wilds. R Rainbird Clarke, reprint, EP Publishing, 1974.
83. The Book of Boswell. Silvester Gordon Boswell, Penguin, 1973.
84. Guide to the Nature Reserves of Norfolk. Norfolk Naturalists' Trust, 1988.

85. Andrew Rogerson, article. Eastern Daily Press, June 17, 1995.

86. The Hedgerows of Tasburgh. Silvia Addington, article, Norfolk Archaeology, vol 37, pt 1, Norfolk & Norwich Archaeological Society, 1978.

87. Background to Breckland. Mason & McClelland, Providence Press, 1994.

88. East Anglia at War, 1939-45. Derek Johnson, Jarrold, 1992.

89. The Village Labourer, 1760-1832. Hammond & Hammond, Longmans Green, 1927.

90. Norfolk In Peril: Highways & Byways. The Norfolk Society (CPRE), 1997.

91. David Higgins, article. The Annual, No 5, Norfolk Archaeological & Historical Research Group, 1996.

92. Montagu Don, article. The Observer, August 10, 1997.

93. Poppyland. Stibbons & Cleveland, Poppyland Publishing, 1981.

94. The Life and Work of Harriet Martineau. Vera Wheatley, Secker & Warburg, 1957.

95. Peddars Way & Norfolk Coast Path. Bruce Robinson, Aurum Press, 1996.

96. Langton's Guide to the Weavers' Way & Angles Way. Andrew Durham, Langton's Guides, 1995.

97. Weavers' Way. Norfolk County Council (Planning & Transportation Department) leaflet, 1996.

98. The Angles Way. Skipper & Williamson, Centre of East Anglian Studies, 1993.

99. Peddars Way & Norfolk Coast Path, accommodation guide. The Ramblers' Association, published annually.

100. Essays of Travel. Robert Louis Stevenson, Chatto & Windus, 1909.

101. Highways & Byways in East Anglia. William A Dutt, Macmillan, 1932.

102. Arthur Cossons, article. Norfolk & Norwich Archaeological Society, Vol. 30, pt 3, 1951.

103. Bloomsbury Dictionary of Word Origins. John Ayto, Bloomsbury, 1991.

104. Rambling On. Mike Harding, Robson Books, 1986.

105. Shanks's Pony. Morris Marples, Country Book Club, 1960.

106. The Rucksack Way. Arthur Sharp, Jenkins, 1934.

107. Newmarket, Bury, Thetford and Cromer Road. CG Harper, publisher unknown, 1904.

108. Country Walking magazine, February, 1998.

109. David Kennett, article. Norfolk Archaeology, vol 36, pt 4, 1977.

110. Robert Halliday, article. Norfolk Archaeology, vol 62, pt 1, 1994.

111. Travellers. The Guardian, Education section, June 15, 1993.

112. Eastern Daily Press. January 10, 1991.

113. Peddars Way and Norfolk Coast Path national trail user survey, summary of results. Norfolk County Council, 1998.
114. Eastern Daily Press. November 14, 1989.
115. Out in the Country, booklet. Countryside Commission, 1985.
116. Eastern Daily Press. August 6, 1954.
117. Eastern Daily Press. February 20, 1998.
118. The Guardian. February 24, 1998.
119. Eastern Daily Press. February 26, 1998.
120. The Observer. March 1, 1998.

ADDITIONAL SUGGESTED READING
A Norfolk Diary. BJ Armstrong, Harrap, 1949.
Claimed by the Sea. Chris & Sarah Weston, Wood Green Publications, 1994.
Bridgwater's Norfolk. Elizabeth Bridgwater, Encompass Press, 1995.
East Anglia Guide. East of England Tourist Board. Published annually.
Fields of Little America. Martin Bowman, Wensum Books, 1977.
Norfolk. Tom Pocock, Pimlico County History Guides, 1995.
Norfolk in the Four Seasons. Ron Wilson, The Lark's Press, 1995.
Norwich. Brian Ayres, English Heritage, 1994.
Peasants & Poachers. Michael Carter, Boydell, 1980.
The Black Fens. A K Astbury, EP Publishing, 1970.
The Norfolk Connection, and, More Norfolk Connections. Keith Skipper, Poppyland Publishing, 1991 and 1992.
The Norfolk & Suffolk Weather Book. Ogley, Davison & Currie, Froglets Publications, 1993.
The Popular Guide to Norfolk Churches, No 1,2,3. Mortlock & Roberts, Acorn Editions, 1981 and 1985.
Wednesday Mornings. Jonathan Mardle, Jarrold, undated.

CONTACT POINTS
Broads Authority, 18 Colegate, Norwich, Norfolk.
Countryside Commission, Eastern Regional Office, Ortona House, 110 Hills Road, Cambridge, CB2 1LQ.
East Anglian Tourist Board, Toppesfield Hall, Hadleigh, Suffolk, IP7 5DN.
English Nature, East Region, 60 Bracondale, Norwich, Norfolk, NR1 2BE.
Forestry Commission, District Office, Santon Downham, Brandon, IP27 OTJ.
National Trust, East Anglia Regional Office, Blicking, Norwich, NR11 6NF.
Norfolk Bus Information Centre, The Advice Arcade, Guildhall Hill, Norwich, NR2 1JH. Tel: 0500 626116.

Norfolk Coast Project, 6 Station Road, Wells, Norfolk, NR23 1AE.

Norfolk County Council (public rights of way enquiries, or Planning and Transportation), County Hall, Martineau Lane, Norwich, NR1 2SG. Tel: 01603 222143.

Norfolk Ornithologists' Association, Aslack Way, Holme next the Sea, Hunstanton, Norfolk, PE36 6LP.

Norfolk Wildlife Trust, 72 The Close, Norwich, NR1 4DF.

Rail Information (for East Anglia, 24 hours). Tel: 0171 928 5100.

Ramblers' Association, 1-5 Wandsworth Road, London, SW8 2XX.

Tourist Information Centre, The Guildhall, Gaol Hill, Norwich. Tel: 01603 666071. (also at Attleborough, Aylsham, Cromer, Diss, East Dereham, Downham Market, Fakenham, Yarmouth, Holt, Hoveton, Hunstanton, King's Lynn, Loddon, Mundesley, Ranworth, Sheringham, Swaffham, Thetford, Walsingham, Watton, Wells, and Wymondham, though some have seasonal opening times).

Youth Hostels Association, South England Region, 11b York Road, Salisbury, Wilts, SP2 7AP.

WEATHER FORECASTS

East Anglian Weatherline: 0891 505308.

Eastern Daily Press Weathercall: 0891 500764.

Norwich Weather Centre, Rouen House, Rouen Road, Norwich, Norfolk, NR1 1RE. Tel: 01603 763898.